Human Heartbeat Detected

Human Heartbeat Detected

essays

❧

Chelsey Clammer

🐓 Red Hen Press | *Pasadena, CA*

Book design by Mark E. Cull

Library of Congress Cataloging-in-Publication Data

Names: Clammer, Chelsey, author.
Title: Human heartbeat detected: essays / Chelsey Clammer.
Description: First edition. | Pasadena, CA: Red Hen Press, [2022]
Identifiers: LCCN 2022021987 (print) | LCCN 2022021988 (ebook) | ISBN 9781636280554 (paperback) | ISBN 9781636280561 (ebook)
Subjects: LCSH: Interpersonal relations. | Human behavior. | Emotions. | Humanity. | American essays.
Classification: LCC HM1106 .C4895 2022 (print) | LCC HM1106 (ebook) | DDC
    302—dc23/eng/20220613
LC record available at https://lccn.loc.gov/2022021987
LC ebook record available at https://lccn.loc.gov/2022021988

The National Endowment for the Arts, the Los Angeles County Arts Commission, the Ahmanson Foundation, the Dwight Stuart Youth Fund, the Max Factor Family Foundation, the Pasadena Tournament of Roses Foundation, the Pasadena Arts & Culture Commission and the City of Pasadena Cultural Affairs Division, the City of Los Angeles Department of Cultural Affairs, the Audrey & Sydney Irmas Charitable Foundation, the Kinder Morgan Foundation, the Meta & George Rosenberg Foundation, the Albert and Elaine Borchard Foundation, the Adams Family Foundation, the Riordan Foundation, Amazon Literary Partnership, the Sam Francis Foundation, and the Mara W. Breech Foundation partially support Red Hen Press.

First Edition
Published by Red Hen Press
www.redhen.org

Literary Acknowledgments

"Carving Out a Community" published in *WOW! Women on Writing: In the Trenches* (2018) *NOTE*: This essay is two different essays spliced together into a lyric essay. The two original essays were: "Cut" (*The Rumpus* 2012) and "Skin and Kin" (*Takkun* 2015). "The Pet Prompt" published by Layla Al-Bedawi (in a personal zine, 2016). *100-Word Story*: "ctrl + alt + delete"; *Atticus Review*: "Balcony, 3 a.m."; *The Flexible Personae*: "Well That Was Awkward as Fuck"; *Foliate Oak*: "June Bugs"; *Gargoyle*: "And that's How You Do It"; *Hip Mama*: "(C)leave"; *Hobart*: "A Slim Sexuality"; *Lamplit Underground*: "Flash Flood"; *Litbreak Magazine*: "One-Hitter"; *Minerva Rising*: "A Seventeen-Pound Surprise Ending"; *Red Fez*: "Puppy Love"; *The Nervous Breakdown*: "The Effects of Silence"; *The Missing Slate*: "Which Is another Way of Saying Decay"; *Oyster River Pages*: "Paddling"; *The Rumpus*: "Detect"; *Sonder Review*: "At a Loss"; *The Stirring*: "What Weeps"; *The Thread*: "It Was Just a Lamp"; and *The Tishman Review*: "Graftology."

For Angela, who held my heart as I jour-
neyed through these essays.
                              —Thanks, love.

                    xo

Contents

Detect

Human heartbeat detected. Welcome, human.

❧

In the grocery store, we try to shop together, both of us armed with a black plastic basket. We weave through my produce section, stroll down his frozen foods aisle. En route from navel oranges to cookie dough ice cream, I say, "Oh! Gotta go grab some salad dressing." He stands. I grab. I return seconds later, his face changed. Staring at the floor, eyebrows raising up and diving down, the musculature of his face in conversation with something I cannot see, something that cannot be heard.

❧

We go to Caribou to get coffee because we've never sat down to write and study here. No camping out at this coffee shop all day, unlike the other establishments we establish ourselves at for hours, one of us plunking away at her experience, the other squinting at articles that raise more questions for him than answers. This Caribou at Twenty-fourth and Hennepin that has the fireplace and the baristas who look like us—young, progressive, educated—is our designated space to *just* get coffee. To just talk. We get coffee. We talk. He shows me a new app on his phone. We laugh as we play memory games, try to guess words with missing letters by their associations with a keyword. TOOTH and AC_E is easy, but H_ART and BEAT brings up too many childhood memories. A pause. We switch to math, then mental agility. Back to laughs. We get up. Leave. What he says in the truck: "I'm sick of it sick of thinking I don't deserve success I can't handle it I'm sick of it I wake up and it's all I can think about *all* I can think like my thoughts aren't my own I'm sick of this shit I can't, I mean how much can . . ." I wait. He ends when he puts his hands to his head. I wait one more beat, then say: "What triggered this?"

Silence.

ॐ

The book on schizophrenia says "split mind." Not "split personality," mind you. The two are different. He is not two different men. Though lately, I have wondered where my husband has been.

ॐ

He built a robot that will only turn on when it detects a human heartbeat. He worked on this robot for days. Months. On and off. Taught himself computer programing and soldering, then how to tweak and tinker in various ways with various wires and breadboards and circuits and others things from companies with names like Adafruit, like Arduino, like mBot.

Micro Center became a frequent destination. He worked on the robot, testing and retesting, programing and reprograming, getting it to talk and move and turn on when sensor and computer and robot all recognized the basics of life. Of being able to be a human. Alive. The heartbeat. For days, months, even now I hear the robotic female voice over and over and over and over as she declares my husband's success at programming software that sparks with life. That he actually activated to life just by being alive himself. Thumbs to sensors, the robot senses his heartbeat, then says what he programmed her to say: "Human heartbeat detected. Welcome, human."

ॐ

I don't want to say "calculated conversations." I don't want to say "I push my needs away." I don't want to admit I can't predict how our interactions will go. But I don't know how else to explain this. How else to describe what it's like to need something—to be heard, listened to—and what it's like to know I have to silence the things I want to say to give space for the thunderstorm of his thoughts that aren't really his own to rumble through, to gust away from his breath, to wait until his eyes clear so I can have a moment when his focus is on me, on the present tense—shall I call it reality?—of the moment in which we are living, together, simultaneously, here, being heard by one another and not interrupted by blasts of thunder. I'm constantly waiting for the weather to clear. They say it's supposed to get nice out, tomorrow.

ॐ

What I'm trying to say is that my husband is fractured. What I want to say is that fractured doesn't mean a death sentence, that it doesn't mean we won't get through this, that fractured is better than shattered, and that we'll be okay, we just have to be aware of the cracks. My concern, though, is that if I actually state, actually point out to him that there *are* cracks, that his mind *is* fractured, that I *am* starting to fissure as well because of the fear of these fractures not being attended to, then we *will* shatter. Superstition led me to leap over sidewalk cracks when I was a kid. My mother never broke her back. I don't think the two are connected, but there's something in this rhyme that speaks to presence of mind, speaks to cracks and concerns and how vigilance is perhaps a way to keep safe. Whole. I worry about what will happen if I point out to him there are bits of him missing. I don't know if this metaphor is working. I'm too tired to finish the figuring.

ॐ

The book says a cold mother is no longer thought to be at fault, but I have witnessed otherwise—how memory games and the mention of "BEAT" ruptures his thoughts, reactions then erupting in our truck. A mother-made madness hammering around inside his head.

ॐ

Each time I need to cry, I wait until he's too involved with his tinkering to want to go outside with me to smoke a cigarette in the –5° evening air. I go outside. I smoke. Sob. Finish up the smoke and the sobs. I have to detach so his detachment doesn't break me. Split me. I go inside with glistening crystals clinging to my eyelashes. He doesn't notice. Keeps tinkering.

ॐ

His mind is a beautiful thing. Even in the splitting. Even in what scares me.

ॐ

A letter I haven't yet written to him: Dear Husband, I can't wait for the day when you read this and find these words amusing—having grown from past madness to present-day structured sanity. That day will denote *growth*. That will mean *healing*. Will mean *recovery*. That we'll be back in that space in which we function together so well—where we can kick back safe, sane, stable, and let go of the absurdities of our past realities.

ॐ

But fault lines originating in his past now ripple into our present. The source of the initial fissure beat into him by his mother. Mental illness and abuse as the catalyst for his cognitive split. Dissociation became a gateway response, one that would eventually lead to my *what triggered this?* wonderings—those fragmented mind moments festering within a history of domestic violence, now spread out by his schizophrenia. I am silenced by his mother, by what she did to him and how it now shapes my marriage into this static silence. Our conversations cut off when he's triggered, when he's distracted by the dialogue going on inside his head. Those hallucinated discussions his mother initiated years ago with a dowel rod from Home Depot.

ə❧

Needing to cry but not wanting to be cold, I take a bath so I can weep without him hearing me. I need to sob some lonelies out of me. My husband is in the other room. I want to say, "My husband's body is in the other room," but that would make it sound like he's dead. He's not. Not really. I plug the tub. Sit down, naked. Then shiver. I turn the faucet. Then fissure.

ə❧

Human heartbeat detected. Welcome, human.

Carving Out a Community

We were the ones who stuck together. The survivors and rioters. Visionary movement makers. Feminist collective, queer contingent—believing the world could be different. We held each other up—symbiotic saviors. Discussed accountability. Discovered the bonds of community.

There, in Chicago, above my bedroom door, the purple-painted wooden sign that said *Intend*. Meaning: harm reduction. Trauma informed. Self-advocate. Boundary setters and keepers. Intentions we set so we could heal from oppression. Live differently. We kept each other strong and empowered, regardless of our struggles. Gave each other care, confidence, and survival. Gave each other that sense of thriving—together.

My community extended beyond my friends as it unfurled throughout the neighborhood in which we lived. Those spaces made of safe, well-lit sidewalks, flourishing community gardens, and the open courtyards of our apartments. Rainbow flags hanging in many windows. This was our little corner of Chicago. The neighborhood—*my* neighborhood—I floated through, peacefully, on that one particular July night. Weaving my way from bar to home, alone, I soon heard a jogger's footsteps barreling down the sidewalk behind me, toward me.

I stepped aside to let him run by, but the end of his run—that finishing line—wasn't beyond me. It was me, my body.

Hands pulling, clawing. I screamed and fought until I finally broke away from his grasp. Then he turned his back to me. Walked away, empty-handed. Violated, the terror of that one-minute interaction became a memory I could never ungrasp. That night, I sobbed my way home, hyperventilating as I walked down the sidewalks of my community that no longer felt like mine. The panic and hypervigilance and anxiety that stemmed from this assault would forever reverberate, ricochet within me, ripple out to my community. Yet stay caged within my skin.

The trauma begins.

આ

There is a decision to cut. It is not a decision. There is a need and there is a desire to make that need go away, to simultaneously want and not want to cut.

The complication here is about how cutting gives you a sense of control, a feeling of letting go. And then later, eventually, after just a few weeks since you started, the cutting begins to control you.

Once I started, I didn't want to stop. No, I did want to. It's that I couldn't. There was a space between my veins and skin that I had to get into—I needed to see what was missing, what didn't feel right. I couldn't resist such disparate pleading, needing to see what was in there, to explore those places where my skin no longer felt attached to my body, no longer enveloped my muscles and tendons, my skeletal system below, beneath it, further down and underneath that hollowed-out sense. It's a space that felt separated from the surface and stifled what was inside it—a struggle to feel alive. I thought the razor could help me find it, that space within myself I could no longer locate, so I carved deep canyons in my skin to empty out my body's memories, hoping I'd find something that would save me. What rose up was a steady stream—rarely a trickle—of blood. My blood. That substance inside me. A part of me now seen. I licked it, yes, *licked* it. It tasted razor-blade metallic. And then past the blood, if I spread open my fresh swipe, I saw translucent flesh and globs of yellow—fat beneath the skin, an inner layer of supposed protection.

I was assaulted on a Sunday and didn't leave my apartment until Wednesday when I went with my feminist friends to tape signs to the sidewalk where I was assaulted. I was terrified of going outside, certain I would be assaulted the second I did—a trauma-induced hypervigilance consumed me—but three days after that Sunday assault, my friends finally coaxed me out of my safe cave, cooked me dinner, and then we took Sharpies to poster boards to do some reclaiming:

"My short dress does not give you the right to grab me."
"He took my safety but not my strength."
"I was assaulted here X on Sunday."
"Protect your community."

My lover even amended a nearby "DO NOT ENTER" street sign:

"DO NOT ENTER someone else's space"

I tried to feel empowered in those moments of sidewalk reclamation and revised signage.

I failed.

There wasn't any hope within me, just the ripple effect of trauma cycling through my skin, having originated from the places where he grabbed my body. It went like this: His touch created physical memories that created flashbacks that created panic attacks that created regrettable drunken razor blade actions that created permanent visual reminders of his touch—his touch created physical memories that created flashbacks that created—

Trauma isn't a linear experience. It loops.

Regardless of the care we held for one another, regardless of the support and strength my community gave me, I still felt scared, anxious, defeated. Deflated. Violated. Flayed, even. Needing to get away from the places he touched, I discovered a strategy to do this. Create a physical sensation to pause it all, to momentarily calm down what was inside my body by controlling its surface. Skin terrorized by the places he struck, I needed to separate myself from it.

I cut.

۶ؤ

The skin is the body's largest organ. It covers the entire body, shields against heat, light, injury, infection. It regulates body temperature and stores water and fat. There are three main layers that compose our flesh. The epidermis is what you see, the solid outer layer that doesn't contain blood vessels. Cut through that and you will run into the dermis. This is where the blood vessels, nerves, and muscles run through the body. Cut even farther down and you hit the subcutaneous fat layer. Here, it is yellow. Here, the flesh turns pulpy and soft. Here, more blood, more nerves.

My skin did not protect me against injury. Against him. Against me. As I cut, I went through my epidermis and dermis, slashed straight down into my subcutaneous layer. All of me was there. Skin layered on top of itself, covered in blood and nerves. I was searching for that empty space I sensed, trying to locate what was missing, what he took. I never found it. Each morning I woke up with pieces of torn fabric tied to my skin, an outer layer of cloth to keep back what was bleeding from within. To protect what was open and raw. Vulnerable.

It failed.

Covered in fresh wounds, I still felt emptied. Within a few instances of razor to skin, I was no longer in control of cutting.

❧

I cut until I needed stitches. Then I cut again. I cut until I had to go to the psych ward, then I got out and then I cut again and then I went back in. When I got out (again), I continued to cut. Wash. Rinse. Repeat. Self-injury is a type of trauma—it, too, loops. I cut enough one early morning that by nightfall I was still bleeding. Sleeping next to my lover, my arm draped over her naked stomach, the sharp lines on my skin dripped, seeped. The feel of self-harm's red liquid woke her up. She stayed calm that night as she wiped clean the places where the cuts had wept onto her abdomen. But soon after, she started her retreat from me. My community followed.

We were the ones who stuck together.

Until we didn't.

We were the ones who supported one another. Until we weren't. Until the stress of supporting me became too much and my community had to break away. Leave. Six months after the assault I was still cutting when they needed to attend to their own struggles and didn't have the energy to continue to attend to mine. Because one friend's sister was in the hell of an active eating disorder. One friend was working to heal from the violence of her last relationship. One was depressed. One was labeled unstable because she wanted to be *he*. Another friend lost her food stamps. Another lost his father. One friend lost her partner.

My community then lost me, severed me, actually. Emptied their hands of me, hoping I would find someone else to hold me up since I still wasn't capable of doing it myself.

೭♦

Suture kits in every hospital contain a similar inventory: antiseptic towelettes, curved hemostat, sterile scalpel blades, surgical probe, operating scissors, suture lip scissors, non-suture wound closure strips, pointed forceps, benzoin swabs, and a spool of black nylon. Hemostats are scissor-looking clamps that hold onto the skin while the sutures are sewn in. Once the wound is numbed by injecting an anesthetic, the nurse prepares the sterilized instruments to bring the skin back together. Although the anesthetic does numb the injury site, you can still feel the pull and tug of flesh as it is sewn shut.

The nurses never asked if I could feel it. Perhaps they did not want to know, didn't want to hear what my answer would have been: an ecstatic, *Yes*.

೭♦

Yes, there was a time that my community did take care of each other, but caring for ourselves was an essential part of that. You can't be a friend to someone if you're not a friend to yourself. Simple as that. My community couldn't help me because I wouldn't help myself. I cut. I wept. I drained their energy, their resilience. Their patience.

How can we be there for someone who has already vacated herself—someone who has left her body because she couldn't escape her memories?

Let go or be dragged.

For their own sanity, their own emotional safety, they turned their backs to me.

Like my assailant, they walked away, left me shattering.

ə♥

Self-harm is believed to be a morbid form of self-help. For people whose emotions are hyper-reactive or for those raised in an emotionally chaotic environment, cutting or creating physical pain feels like the best way to silence anxiety, to shut out memories. After surviving a traumatic situation, a person will often relieve the reactionary anxiety with physical harm. Like popping a balloon, the anxiety seems to just go away.

I do not remember my first cut. I do not know what made me take that initial swipe. I know I was drunk. I know it quickly became my nightly routine.

Then I cut so badly (again) that I needed to get stitches (again). It would be the fifth time in less than a year that a nurse had to pull out the suture kit upon my arrival. By then, the fascination had worn off. Watching the suturing was still interesting but no longer exciting. Actually, it was more like routine, shuffling its feet toward the mundane. This last time, though, I wasn't drunk when I cut, but hungover. I drank the night before. I cut the night before. When I woke up feeling raw, hopeless, still stuck in a well of depression and still friendless, I did what I thought would assuage it. I cut.

The cut finally hurt.

ə♥

There is a certain type of silence that permeates a psych ward's hallways at 2:00 a.m. It's comforting, safe because life's chaos doesn't exist when in a secluded and locked unit. Since the support I needed was beyond my community's capabilities, I cut my way towards needing the professionals—those who had the resources to stitch me up and help calm me down—to swoop in and save me.

The psych ward protected me from the razor. Once removed, I realized I had been trying to figure out the story of my experience, of my body, with swipes and slices. But the cuts only silenced me, cut me off from my community. I had to find a different way—one that didn't harm me—to put language to my pain.

This is about more than bodies. It's about voices, stories. It's about the space needed to explore those voices, those stories. To put words to what feels incomprehensible. *Why this? Why me?* To feel someone is listening. I needed that space in which I was supported by people, not forced to be fixed. It was about understanding. About letting me return to myself in my own way, in my own time. It was about writing my story of survival in my own terms, my own words. Without a community to talk to, I turned to writing.

I had adjectives and verbs, had stories built inside me full of metaphors and allusions and specific words that wanted to be heard. The stillness and safety of the psych ward gave me the space to write the pain out of me, to put down the razor and pick up a pen.

So that's what I did.

I put down the razor.

I picked up a pen.

I inked my way towards repairing the ruins my life had become.

ə♥

Writing was a process of discovering. Each time I wrote, I found a new angle into my past, a new way to approach and consider life. It was about getting that narrative out. Words as ushers. I wasn't so much documenting trauma, but transforming past pain into a tangible story. Surviving this life is an art. If I didn't tell my story, the traumatic memories would keep replaying in my mind—a continuous loop of what I wished I could leave behind but couldn't get out of me. No matter how harsh and harrowing the words were, I had to write them out to cultivate some understanding about who I was—and especially who I was without my community, how they had to continue without me. How I could do the same without them.

I was turning pain into art. Crafting it. Gaining strength by inciting a voice.

Ten days after I checked myself into the psych ward, I was ready to leave and emotionally equipped to let that voice be heard. Writing was a way to see it all, right there in front of me, on the page, and I knew that I needed some witnesses, knew that I wanted other people to see what I had created so I could keep cultivating my voice. Keep discovering myself.

I discovered a different community, one that knew how to listen, how to care for me by encouraging self-exploration through writing. By volunteering to read submissions for a nonfiction literary journal, I was able to witness other people's stories. My new community spawned. There were the writers and editors I worked with at the journal, then the online writing groups I joined and the friends I made through them. Then more writers and editors I met by submitting my work for publication and eventually entering into a low-residency MFA program—my new community was snowballing into something amazing. Exciting. Sturdy. I had found my tribe of people who would never walk away from me, even if there was too much pain and not enough healing going on in my life. No, these writers became the ones who encouraged me to speak more about that pain, to find new ways to write about it, new ways to heal from it. I encountered writers who told me to roll up my sleeves and dive right into those darkest moments of my existence. Don't avoid. Don't be scared. Don't give up and walk away. Go deep. Excavate beyond the cuts. Exhume as the scars form.

Having figured out how to attend to myself, I could finally be there for someone else. I could create that co-healing space. I could share my writing, could read. Listen.

ॐ

My new community exists in my Google contacts, my friend lists, my connections. We "follow" each other in non-stalker ways. We learn even more of each other through publications and reviews and interviews. The rough drafts friends send me. The emails I send them asking for opinions on punctuation. We are all one email, one post, one website away. Many of the people I consider my best friends are women I've never met in person. But we don't need to be in the same physical space to feel the strength of friendship and the community of which we're all a part.

We are the ones who stick together as we read each other's work, the ones who know and share the power of words.

In Minneapolis, Marya writes about mental illness. In Seattle, Bernard writes about drug addiction. Kristina writes about painful tragedies in Philadelphia, and Abe in Austin unsilences the secrets of incest. Melissa explores independence and freedom from domestic violence as she scrawls down words in Michigan, crafting her memoir. In Tel Aviv, Morgan reckons with her body. Tayyba in Houston figures out her American identity.

I read my friends' stories as I continue to put words to my own.

There's a type of encouragement that flows from each sentence, each story. Readers witness our painful experience. They face the trauma with us, tell us to keep going, that we have a right to tell our stories. How a word after a word puts us back into the world.

We are the ones who craft language and let it flow so that we can let go. Connect.

We stitch our stories together, never cutting out or cutting off what feels too harsh—that place where we know our narratives begin.

Well That Was Awkward as Fuck

Indeed. We're standing on the sidelines of the Women's March on Austin. We're here not because we want to join in on the marching—I mean, we're feminists for sure, but a bit ambivalent about the current protesting tactics, knowing that attendance no longer gets you credit. We're here because Husband wants to record some footage for his travelogue about Texas and I want to see two women we knew in college and haven't talked to in over a decade. Last week, they Facebooked that they were going to attend the march and we said we'd see them there. We're here, at this pep rally, because we feminists in this country are still marching and have yet to learn that marching more or less achieves jack shit—these formulaic and police-maintained "March for [insert cause here]" all need to get extinct already, because we the people gathering to show the government we don't agree with their insanities no longer creates a forward change like it used to, and therefore all that we're really doing is marching in place. Anyway. Here we are at the Women's March on Austin, mazing our way through the sea of people in pink pussy hats to locate two women and the wife of one of them. It's exciting to see people from way back when because reunions give me an opportunity to show off just how fucking cute Husband and I are together because that's just how vain I am.

We further make our way to the outskirts of the pussy-headed parade and then I hear my name. I turn around and see these past friends sitting on their blanket with an apparent lack of reunion excitement because after they see us and we see them, they stay seated—which isn't to say that *all rise* when we arrive. Still. It's called a greeting. They continue to look at us, motionless. Regardless, I do a little giddy walk to them and throw a zest of pep in my step because at this point I'm still believing reunions rock. When Husband and I are a few steps away, they collectively decide to stand, slowly. Unceremoniously. I dive in for some hugs because that's what friends do when they haven't seen each other for forever and a day. First hug is good, second one is weird, and then I face the wife-stranger and we do a short hug because everyone else is hugging, though by the time I step back from our vague embrace I have already forgotten her name.

Post-hugs, post-hellos, post-*how ya doin's* and the *how's life* conversation fillers, the five of us just kind of stand around and mumble other updates. After one lull in the conversation, we look out at the crowd like bored adults who are realizing that the game they loved to play during recess is no longer fun or interesting. We quickly revert to pulling out our cell phones/safety blankets to show off some pictures. And then the lull re-arrives and we go back to looking at what democracy supposedly looks like. One of the women pushes into the blank space of our dwindling conversation, "Well. We should get going soon . . ."—a statement fully infused with an "aw-shucks" tone of faux-disappointment. We look at some more pictures so as to appear that of course there's no desire rising up in any of us to bolt from this textbook-awkward situation. Then, a few more flashes of reminiscences followed by an empty invitation to join them for lunch, the subtext of which is *I don't want you to come but I don't want to look like an asshole for not inviting you.* Stupid pleasantries. Husband and I respond with, "Oh cool! Yeah, maybe." And then, finally, a final hug. Goodbye.

Marching back to our truck, the shroud of *what in the fuck?* descends on mine and Husband's conversation. We don't know why what happened just happened, why we felt weird around people we used to see every day in college—people I've kissed when drunk, people whose cars I've cleaned out puke from even when the puke hadn't geysered from my own mouth the night before, how these women were at of all the parties I attended, they were women who witnessed all the dumb drunk shit I did, women whose voices I've screamed along with at previous women's rights marches and anti-war protests and gay rights demonstrations—female empowerment thrumming out each time we collectively answered, "When do we want it?!?" Now, eleven years later—and thirteen years after the last women's march we attended together—it's at this current ineffective show of hands that we experience an ineffective reunion.

"Well that was awkward as fuck," I comment.

We don't know why the statement I say is true, just that it is.

Wait. Scratch that. Maybe we do know. Maybe it's because we actually didn't know each other all that well. Maybe it's because we were never really that close to begin with—maybe alcohol + similar interests ≠ bff.

Or:

"Maybe we stunned them into silence by just how fucking cute we are!" I say this not because I'm vain, but because that's just my way of avoiding this particular reality. How it is that once-active relationships can devolve into stagnancy, into friendships with no futures, our past fondness for each other just marching in place, weary.

The Pet Prompt

Prompt: Have you ever had the rotten experience of having to put a pet down?

I thought that said *pen* not *pet* so I high-fived the prompt and thought, "Finally! Somebody *gets* me!" Because yes, many times—daily, actually—I've had the rotten experience of having to put a pen down. And every time I click the pen's end, its .7 point sucked back into its cylindrical body, is an act that sucks as much as it always has. Because *pen down* means life returns to its unwavering routines and unreasonable perspectives. *Pen down* means stop writing and start obsessing over stressors, like my body, like how I can't look in the mirror and think, "pretty." A downed pen is distraction's end—mind jerked from crafting thoughts to assessing flesh. Mine. All of it.

A friend once said I needed to treat, love, and care for my body like it was my pet. It's a curious concept, especially for me—a woman who takes every frustration out on her body. No one is a fan of animal cruelty. But let's say I misheard this friend like I misread this prompt, i.e., "Treat, love, and care for your body like it was your pen." I respect pens. Love them. Drool over them. I've actually said, "You've met my pens," and it took more than a few moments to realize *I really just said that*. Though it raises a good point—have I ever met my body?

Yes. I think. If the body is a pet, a pen, a tool used to get to know who I am, then yes, my body is a pen. I've met her. And I keep putting her down.

Graftology

Here, skin's story.

Snatched & trapped & grabbed & the escape & the flash-backs & the re-living & the re-living & surviving & please no not again & again with the ampersand, & there's still more to tell. & how could this be? There will always be more to tell. Always.

What's the lifespan of an ampersand?

& how I thought he was a midnight jogger. & how I didn't raise my hackles & how now my shoulders carry the weight of an ampersand & how there's self-inflicted misplaced blame on my body & how it stems from that too-short dress & how the blame bullies me & how I berate my body for thinking it could wear something so revealing.

Stop.

Leave me alone.

Find my voice.

Pen and paper.

Of what meaning is our body when we funnel flesh into writing? What words do we use to locate our meanings? How to create a language of letters from this form I have yet to fully feel? A body of work. Fonts fill a page, inhabit the blank spaces, & thoughts fill in the places in between my cells. Inhabiting my body, I try to read what's written here. On me. The misconceiving surface full of the *I'm okay* myth. & there's the inner truth we don't quite know how to explain.

Not yet.

Learning language.

A story waiting to be written.

& how there is so much more to read. Always.

The lifespan of an ampersand.

❧

Graphology

Funneled into the landscape of a letter. A single letter. And how a word supposedly reveals even more about me. Textual unveiling. So think, then, about the power of an entire sentence. This sentence, for instance. So much of me is supposedly here, in this handwriting. I inhabit words so vividly. Such energy. Personality siphoned into the look of these letters. Letters like skin. The surface layer that feeds assumptions. As if my letters are proof that I'm living. But what if I know the rules for how to read the elements of handwriting? This is me mis-guiding. I make my longhand letters look like they are uncovering my core. I intentionally pivot the reader's attention away from my pith, from what's hiding behind crafted reflections. I make my writing spike with verticle words. How this is just an act, a role I perform to cover up the consequences of a short dress that didn't cover enough.

& feet stomping & footfalls rushing up behind me & how that sound will always echo through me & my memories & this body & how this body doesn't seem like itself anymore & how it's not & how it won't ever & will never again hear the supposed-language of safety. It no longer exists.

& there's more.

Always.

Graphology: The study of handwriting to find clues that can figure out one's character.

Some factors:

1. **Size**: large handwriting as in over-confident, as in *I hold all the power.* Extra small as in a possible indication of uncertainty, as in *why I am alive?* (And the correlations I could create here.) (Why me?) (How could I let him overpower me?) (What reduced me to an eyeful of flesh?) (No more me, please.) (Get away from me, please.) (Now the skin's negative space.) (Now the eating disorder thriving and the body leaving.) (Now not enough body here to grab.)

2. **Slant**: type of tilt. Trajectory. Handwriting slanting left means holding back. Slanting right means forward-thinking. Ruminative of the past or inquisitive of the future? And then there's the right here, the in this moment. No swaying. No slant. Pure vertical letters. Assure. Assuaged.

3. **Pressure**: life force and energy flow. Libido. Physiological energy. The intellectual vitality of the intensely bold writing. The hard-pressed *I got this.* Or the hesitation of the light, longhanded *not me.* Mental

decay. The words slipping away. Invisible. Normalcy is found between these two extremes. Easily seen. Readable. Adapted to stress. And triggers. Life is only transitory. Always. Because pressure will forever oscillate. Each experience shifts. Even the ones we can live with. Yes, *all is well*. Thank you for asking. & the strive to stay steady when *I'm doing okay* means nothing. A filler for an inquiry. Normalcy.

(& after his grasp & after my gasp & how the gasp sounded so strikingly startled & then deep chills & then an instant it hits & I know I'll never know safety again & my life moves away from its normal and carefree state & how right there & then the dark crashed in.)

Look up at that opening segment, at that writing (& its intentionality). Let's look at this:

Size: medium   —practical

Slant: vertical   —present

Pressue: balanced   —adapted

Here, my letters are thoughtful. Steady. Content with where I am. Who I am. Settled. Like I'm at home now, in my body. I'm not accustomed to this, to adaptability, such a lowered level of stress, an intention to encourage good health. This is what my handwriting says.

Here is a good place to be.

Balanced.

Home.

Indeed.

However.

My memories of being grabbed & assaulted & startled all lead me to vacate my body; all create my trauma history. & it's not just about that stranger who grabbed me one night while I was walking home alone. & it's not just about how when I got home after I walked those five long Chicago city blocks with hyperventilation & sobs choking me & hands shaking too much to get the keys to settle in my fingers & they weren't steady & I wasn't steady, & after a door finally unlocked, I flung my body into my home that no longer felt like mine. Something was missing. That "safety."

& how I felt hollow.

& how the hollowness of my home is here.

Graphology is contingent upon another matter. Sign here. No signature to analyze along with longhand? Then the meaning is unbalanced, only half there.

> The surface shows survival. Good. Neat. Acceptable. Now, as of this writing, everything feels adaptable and practical and how I can take care of myself thank you very much, and how this longhand confirms that. See? I'm being perfectly clear. A perfectly good liar. Because those pen strokes are controlled, intentional. They silence what's inside, but can't figure out how to stop that play back loop of how he wanted to know my name.

Such thoughtful longhand. Present. Tranquil. Fake. The surface layer of *all is well.*

Now sign here.

Damn it.

Revelation. De-curtaining. Un-hiding. Below the surface of words, the roots of sanity are

Keep my head above water.

I can do this. I can breathe just fine.

But the silt of that lie rages under it, lies within me.

The truth: Post-Traumatic Stress Disorder. The symptoms inside my body I can't fully cover. The ways in which I hurt, hurt me. A fissured foundation. My letters should be small, slant back. Faint. But I can control all of that. You know this.

This is where the signature comes in.

A full meaning cannot be gathered if a signature isn't present. We need it to compare. Controlled handwriting slays the signs that something inside me is decaying. The signature, though, is harder to control. It's personal. An avenue for expression. & what festers within.

For example:

Precise letters and spastic signature—practiced calm to cover inner turmoil.

Bold writing and a light signature—now hide.

Writing and signature are the same—what you see is what you get.

I'll further make my point by letting you see me:

I'm an independent woman, all practical and determined.

But:

[signature]

My signature.

Size: large—I cannot hide from myself, regardless.
 Slant: right—who will grab me next? When?
 Pressure: bold—so emotionally intense, distressing. Not even(ly) adapted.
 See? Signature directly opposes my handwriting. I am nullified. Numb. Complex even though I present as simple.
 I'm funneled into a space I constantly create.

I fit inside the space of a letter.

> Dear body,
> I'm slowly learning your language, translating your text so you won't be so foreign to me, so we can live here, together, amicably. Like before he ran up behind me. I would like to think that one day I'll return to liking you. To wanting you.

Either way, I'm doing okay.
 Right?
 No. Not with the following revelation.
 Sincerely,

[signature]

ॐ

Self-Expression

The ampersand & how it continues to assault my body.

& how when I finally got home that night, I realized I no longer lived there.

& how the concept of "home" ceased existence.

Later, after a while, I looked for my story & hunted down a language that could describe all of this & me & how words vacated my body & how initially, for a while, my story didn't know its own identity, its own telling.

Poetics. Here I am. Stanzas sticking out. Yet also elusive. Skin speaking. Like always. Strength in how I string my own words together. Identity. But back then the written language failed. No words to describe this_____. So instead of putting pen to paper, I expended my energy on a different kind of writing, one to transform initial impressions, to make meaning of the recent past events, to ignore the risks of a certain type of self-expression. Permanence. *I needed this.* To learn how to pronounce who I was. My story. There was more. Always.

& body became canvas & a physical language unfurled. Or, rather, slashed.

Screams & clenched fists & arms now rising & the air full of self-defense & disbelief & defeat & he asks me, *hey baby what's your name* & I don't tell him & I say no & then more screams & then I say, *leave* & I then say, *leave now* & his eyes penetrate my body & a few moments later he walks away, calmly.

& I break.

Signature cuts.

Size. Slant. Pressure. Size, slant, pressure. Size slant pressure. Sizeslantpressure. The mantra in my head coils together, tighter, quickly tightens and coils and tightens and coils and tightens together too quickly, so quick that it takes a bit for me to realize what's really going on. How one style of my writing has a roughness. Notches with permanence. Years of tough moments. Notated.

I cut.

Not now. Not in this moment. Not in any moment in the past eleven years. I'm talking past tense cutting here. No razor blade in my hand for over 4,015 days. Nothing with a sharp point pressed into my skin. No pulling my hand in one quick, swiping motion across the landscape of my forearm. Now the narrative, the scars—such rough writing—are on my skin saying how back then the edges of my sanity frayed and tore at a frightening pace.

The lines marking the territory of my trauma, its story published on my skin. Before this no cuts, no need to flay.

& then.

& then sharp razor art to confirm the rough moments. The past tense will forever be present. (Here I am.) (Here with these scars.) Cuts created to counteract trauma triggers, to silence the incessant hypotheticals.

What if I had turned around when I heard someone running up behind me? What if I had stayed at the bar for one more drink? Or left the bar one drink earlier? What if I hadn't broken up with my girlfriend ten days prior? What if something worse had happened? What if I had told him my name? What if he had actually raped me?

What if the next stranger does?

What if I never make it home?

Silence is violence, so I had to tell my story to extinguish my pain.

I took the razor and held on tight. I started writing.

Size. Slant. Pressure.

The graphology of self-harm.

At first I couldn't quite translate what the cuts spoke of. I vagued my way through the cutter cliché. What else was there to think? To do? Eradicate the emotionless. Sure. It was a way to tell a tale when I didn't know what else to say. Now, though, I have found a way to unriddle my past, to read the scars' stories.

- Size
- Slant
- Pressure

Three inches long and at a 45° angle from the inner crook of my left elbow, lies the biggest scar—thick and jagged. It shows how hard I pressed. The thickness of the purple scar a testament to how deep that handmade canyon was, the distance my self-parted skin had to traverse for my flesh to come back together again.

The size, slant, and pressure of each wound points to my past identity: cutter.

Roll call:

1. One big bright white line my underwear hides—
   medium length and chromatic lightness. Not a serious
   cut, though descending. The scar reads as practical,
   pessimistic, hesitant. *Is this what I want to do?*

   My need to un-numb? Sure. Why not? Yup. Here,
   you go: the vague cutter cliché.

2. Too many nicks on my fingers to count on two hands. Their shapes, inconsistent. Specks, flecks of light scars littering my fingers. Analysis: cerebral, unsettled, involuntary.

    This isn't what I want to do.

    But what else was there?

3. Three jagged scars on my hands like thick branches that slightly sway. They're medium in length and waver around, resistant to form a straight line. Heavy though indecisive. Active. *When will I stop? How?*
    Truth: there is no past tense for *heal*.

4. There are more. Seventy-nine more scars to address.
    What am I? Victim? Survivor?
    Cutter.

I'm a witness, my flesh a testament to ampersanding's endurance. Six years later & still the haunting. & still it keeps going & still going & still going & never gone. & etc. & this means there is always more. Always.

Ampersanding.

Like writers, cutters prefer to work alone on their craft. Solitude. Quiet time to figure out what it is we want to say. Each writer has her own style, her own history of how she started writing. At the time, I didn't know why I wrote those first lines, first phrases, and sentences of slices. I didn't know what they meant. I hadn't figured that out yet. So I just went with it. Let the razor do the figuring, the sharing. We all have to start somewhere. And look how far I've come. Eighty-eight stories about my past troubles. Right here. Just look at them. Permanence. Public knowledge.

My skin gives me away.

My body, a home in which my past can't reside. Hide.

৵

Graftology

Alone & walking & two eyes laser-ing in on me & how they cut & dart through the dark to find me. The silent eyes, the spotlight-like stare, that man's eyes zeroing in on me. & this is no longer about sight, but geography. & then there will be a part of me missing.

Now, think blood. Think: large and a lot. Think: gaping wound. Think: metaphor. How the point of skin is to protect all that's underneath it. But what if there's too much wound for the torn skin to join hands again? Enter: a slice from somewhere else. A large bandage of human skin. Transplanted from an intact part of the body to the wound site. This is called a skin graft. The added layer of skin protects against infection, but only if it has self-acceptance, if the fringes of flayed flesh don't reject the thin patch of skin that's only there to help.

The vocabulary of injury is universal. The alphabet of sound assumptions. The language of pain hithers when inner layers are flayed. Displayed. Observable.

He watched me that night, ran up behind me, ecstatic to shake more than my hand.

Later, *What happened? How'd you get that scar?*

Skin Grafting 101:

Away from the site of physical trauma, where a sizeable chunk of skin is missing, a layer of skin is removed from this different locale and affixed to said open wound with stitches and/or staples. Dress the effects of torn-away flesh with a piece from its intact self, found in its wardrobe of human skin. Once stretched, stitched, stapled, the healthy skin starts glugging plasma, starts watering the blood vessels so they'll stick to ragged edges. Then blossom. Flourish. A physical trauma corrected with a thin sheet of itself, handmade.

The scar is fierce. Large. Unavoidable.

Like the angry self-inflicted ones.

But there's a difference.

Tool found, then used. Oh no. Went deeper than I meant to. Call a friend. *Can you drive me to the ER?* And then, there I am, in my own curtained-off room, stripped of my possessions, an hour-long assessment for how much of a harm I am to myself (this is not about the others). Then, the stitches. Finally. This regret and source of shame can come to a close.

People aren't supposed to do these things to their skin.

I am secluded by assumptions. Shunned. Fierce scars so unavoidable. And so at times, covered. Hidden. Sweatshirts worn regardless of heat. Thick cotton under a hot sun spotlight my woman-made injuries underneath.

That's one story.

Here's the other:

Action. Accident. Crash. Blood. When you arrive at the ER with an accidental wound, your medical needs will be attended to *immediately*, because the dam broke and the blood reservoir is waterfalling out and the infection is crawling in. The surgeon hurries, scrubs up, transforms from Doc to medical ambassador. She translates skin trauma to a healed version of itself with a donation from another location.

Then, an ugly patch of scarred skin created. Gruesome, yes, yet easier to look at than the self-inflicted thin ones that show so much more.

People and their stares.

What happened to your arms?

I never said this was going to be pretty.

& I don't want to talk about it anymore.

The language of silence.

The home uninhabited.

& it's not that we can't hear it. It's not that we don't want to hear it. It's not that we're ignoring it. It's not that we don't understand it. & it's not that we don't want to come in, settle down.

Trauma happens.

Move on.

But:

There's the irreversible fact of pain published on flesh.

Here, I don't know if I'm speaking of skin grafts or self-harm.

It depends on intentions.

Art

Here, I intend to make meaning.

I am a walking collection of syllables. An anthology of images.

Volumes of letters.

A home waiting to be admired. Loved.

This body.

& its skin.

Skin speaks. Scars are easy to hear, though hard to listen to. The ugliness of their obviousness. The screaming evidence of a mistake. How to hear the meaning behind them, those stories I didn't know how to start. Approach.

Languageless.

Now, images. There are other stories, stories that shifted from pain to presentation. Images on my skin. Tattooed identity. These images have healed beautifully. Each pinprick of ink is a piece of my story's art. The picture book of my body. It's meaning. It's healing. & how the look of *fierce* has finally vagued. A hushed just hue.

My body is composed of paper, with scribblings, those initial attempts to tell my story that appear on the surface layer of myself. All that can be judged, marked, edited and torn is waiting there to be read. A palimpsest of texts, my body stacks up layers, grows into chapters. Meaning accumulates.

But there's also this:

See the skin boundary broken, again, but with art? Beauty. Tattoos—science ones, specifically. I flip through a book of science tattoos, and what seeps into my sight are images of what we share inside us, printed on top of the fleshy boundaries—outside skin revealing what's in. How science art inked in skin shows us the art of our bodies' science, the images that un-curtain the concept of what lives within.

The Tattoo Gallery

Picture #1: DNA

Lines helix up his spine. Shades of gray representing the

blueprints of our bodies. The DNA twists north, up his spinal cord. Under the surface of this building block of self lies what makes him. What grows within him. And us. Outside, that spiral up his spine. Inside, the carousel of chemistry making his body a living thing.

Like the tree his helix tattoo grows into. The branches branch out in the middle of his back, bridge shoulder blade to shoulder blade. There are roots, too. The base of his DNA planted into the surface of his lower lumbar. The timber. Its life.

The element that makes his life inside becomes a part of his outside, visible. Inked. His canvas. The roots of us, of him twirling up to tree branches with leaves that mean many things. Such as life. Growth. Life cycle. Sustenance. And the texture is there, too—that feel of being a living, shifting thing.

Picture #2: Serotonin

Now, a woman's back. Another element of life living between two shoulder blades. (And I think of that word, remember how a blade let me see inside, guided me as I tried to understand this skin. The alive.) The life of her tattoo goes deeper than DNA.

It's not just a matter of chemistry or biology. This is about geometry. Hexagon. Pentagon. Right angles. Obtuse, too. Black lines. Thick. No shading.

A few letters and a subscripted "2" tells those who know this language that the tattoo is the shape of what keeps the happy here.

Serotonin.

Found underneath each layer of self lies the structure of moods. The essence of emotions, now seen on her skin.

Is this tattoo a belief in, or a plea for positivity? Serotonin is the chemical that, in its essence, makes us happy. But what of this tattoo's location on her body? Spread across her back, a placement meaning she perhaps will never see it. Has she turned her back on happiness? Will she ever forget what's back there, on her skin? In her body? Her serotonin. Hopefully not. The necessity of happy. Though this isn't about *if* she can or cannot remember these things, but how her skin *is* empowered to keep on living. The properties of serotonin tattooed on her back. Yes, they have her back.

Picture # 3: Home

Here I am. This one's mine.

The language living in me helps to heal the places where he put his hands on me, in me.

This is what I know: not just what my tattoo means, but how it felt to have the word *home* pressed, poked, needled into my skin. My body is marked with many inked images. Sixteen, as of this writing. But this one, here, toward the top of my right arm, the deltoid shaping the skin that stretches over it. This is where I've decided to find my home—right here, in my body.

To house myself.

To be at home in myself. With myself. Cozy up. I wear my home on my sleeve.

"Home" tattooed near my shoulder (though not the blades).

Welcome.

I put the tattoo of the word *home* on a place I can easily see. This is about safety. The words help you read me. Home because my body houses my history. How I'm figuring out how not to just tell my story, but how to live with it. In it. Which is to say I'm learning to feel at home in my body.

And the font used:

"The letters [of Papyrus] have notches and roughness, and give a good account of a chalk or crayon fraying at the edges."
—Simon Garfield

Touch me & the edges of my safety will fray.

Papyrus breaks away like granite. Crushed like gravel. Not fully developed. But it's beautiful. Strong. Letters crumble but they're still there. Existing in the best way they can. It's this perspective on Papyrus that made my *home* complete. Yes:
home
& I'm still here, regardless of his hands.
& I have staked residence in myself.
& the renovations.
& this is about intentions.
& there's still more to tell.
(Always.)
(Always there will be more to tell.)
Always.
& I want to tell you I've finally come home.
&:

"This is the best thing about the ampersand—its energy, its refusal to sit still."
—Simon Garfield

&

The Effects of Silence

"I have a secret," David said. Then, silence. No secret spilled. Not for another three months.

Next, his outbursts, explosions of anger. Throwing glass on the floor, acting up at home, punches thrown, and he goes to preschool with the same attitude—rage snapping at random. He still couldn't say what he had to say, but actions, of course, speak louder than words. When a four-year-old throws his puppy across the backyard, it's hard not to hear how he needs to speak.

But there's the fact of that antiquated thought, a belief born and raised in the Victorian era, one that has sustained centuries of adherence: *Children should be seen, not heard.*

In other words, this ageist slogan says children are inherently unruly. Disruptive. Each one of them. And rude. Absolutely. They run around restaurants and twirl around stores, cartwheel down aisles breaking every social more, every code of conduct we've put in place to police our interactions. Kids are inconsiderate and cause breakables to crash to the floor because they insist on seeing with their hands, not with their eyes.

But we were all children at one point—have all experienced the ways in which kids are shushed. We all know how it feels to be seen as just a kid who gets on adults' nerves, especially when shouting just to be heard. So what's a kid to do if he needs to speak up? Speak out? What's a kid to do when an adult sees him with more than just his eyes, when he doesn't keep his hands to himself, and then he tells the kid not to tattle—or else? Violence suspended in the onslaught of his silence.

A child is told to speak up about abuse, even though he's instructed not to be heard. This is where a new type of listening comes in. The boy finds his voice through his body, his movements incited by his anxiety rising. See that bizarre and troublesome behavior? Something had to have happened.

And something had to have led up to that moment when the puppy left David's hands and soared across the length of their backyard. Prior to this telling gesture, Emma had been concerned about her four-year-old son's behavior. "David had been saying that he and my ex had secrets together. He had been breaking glass all over the house and was having severe separation anxiety that kept escalating." But David still wouldn't tell. Without her son speaking up about his secrets—his mind knotted in indecision about what was safe to say, what wasn't, what would happen if his secrets were spoken—the only clues Emma could listen to were those expressed through his actions. "He was having severe nightmares, couldn't sleep alone, and was peeing on himself," she explains. It was obvious that David had something to say but didn't know how to say it, or perhaps was too frightened to tell. As her son continued to act out—dragging his older sister, Hannah, across the floor and punching her tooth out—Emma put her son in therapy. Still, only his actions spoke.

Then he threw the dog and then Hannah screamed and then Emma ran out to the backyard and asked him what was going on. "He said he didn't want to tell me," Emma explains. "After sitting in timeout and crying silently, he then said, 'Okay, I really have to tell you something.' I told him no, that he needed to tell his therapist. Then he said, 'No Momma, I really have to tell you something.'"

Okay. Go.

What do you do when your four-year-old son tells you that your ex-boyfriend took him into the bathroom?

"And then what happened?" Emma asked David.

What do you say when your four-year-old son tells you that your ex-boyfriend then peed on him?

"And then what happened? Emma asked again.

What do you do with this response: "Why was his pee white, Momma?"

"And then what happened?" Emma kept going, not answering her son's question, not wanting to risk his talking to stop. "And then what happened?" Emma asked and asked and asked until her son said definitively, "And then I went out and played."

In that moment, Emma hugged David, told him nothing was his fault.

Now, two years later, her son's words are still burned into her brain. "I tried to get in touch with his therapist and my lawyer," Emma says. "We knew something had been wrong, but I wasn't prepared for that. I didn't know what to do."

Because, yes, what do you do when your son finally speaks, when you at last know that *what happened next* was a sexual assault?

❧

In his article, "Seen and Not Heard," David Wilson explains,

"We don't listen to child victims or know how they have tried to overcome abuse because we don't listen to children. . . . We want our children as passive, quiet, grateful, designer accessories to suit our needs and to reflect well on our sense of self."

Who wants their sense of self to be bogged down by someone else's trauma? No one. Enter the trauma- and truth-avoidant trilogy: ignore, deny, deflect.

"Right from the very beginning, people doubted me and accused me of coaching my kids to say these things," Emma explains. "Law enforcement has refused to explore the case in any way. They aren't listening."

By acknowledging a child's outcry, by listening when a kid says he was sexually assaulted, by believing that a mother is protecting and not coaching her children, we put ourselves in the position where we have to not only listen and respond, but also recognize a frightening and sickening fact: We are a species that rapes and abuses our offspring.

So disregard *stranger danger.*

We keep it all in the family now.

David is the middle child of the family. He and Hannah, conceived via IVF, have the same donor father, but Esther, his younger half-sister, was an unplanned result from what should have been a rebound relationship. And although Emma only dated the man for five months—which, taking into account his abusive tendencies and bizarre behavior, was, in hindsight, five months too many—she was already in the process of separating herself from this man when she found out she was pregnant.

With blue-green eyes and fuller lips, Esther's physical features aren't shared with her two older siblings. She gets it from her father, who is also the person who will rape her. In 2014, a year after Esther is born, the man is "kind enough" to agree to babysit Emma's kids one summer while she's at work, which is when he starts sexually assaulting his daughter and her siblings. This is when David's behavior first started to decline. How he'd frequently scream and cry when Emma had to leave in the morning. By the end of the summer, Emma separated herself as much as possible from Esther's father, who seemed to be the source of every problem. A court-ordered visitation schedule was put in place and Emma made sure to follow it—taking all three kids to McDonald's so the father could spend time with Esther and her tag-along siblings. Within the next year, David began to have apparent PTSD episodes during the supervised visitations until it was abundantly clear that something was going on—though what? More PTSD episodes occurred, including that one climatic afternoon when David threw his puppy across the backyard.

From the moment of that first outcry, Emma sought out ways to keep her kids safe—but no one has yet to deliver their services and support. Child Protective Services questioned the kids, "but it wasn't until I took them to the Child Advocacy Center that they were actually interviewed about trauma," says Emma. This act is representative of all of Emma's actions and interactions: When dealing with under-staffed and under-funded state and government organizations and departments, you have to become your own advocate for any initiative to be taken. Unless you have a degree in child trauma, you will be uncertain as to if you are taking the right steps at the right time—if you are doing the right thing in the right way.

"You play all of the events over and over and over in your head because you're a mother," Emma says. "I ask myself what

I could have done differently. I did everything I was told to do—I put them in therapy and didn't influence their opinions or memories. I want to understand how it is that a kid can make a very clear outcry from the very beginning, and nothing has happened that actually protects him."

From this lack of protection, Emma did the best thing she could to ensure her children's safety: she applied to and received a job offer at an out-of-state Ivy League college.

Once they were safe and states away from David's abuser, Esther then made her first outcry about how The Monster hurt her. Esther's outcry: He touched her private parts while she was in a hotel room with him during his first eight-hour unsupervised visit. In their new home state, Emma continued to fight for her children. She immediately set up meetings with the college's safety administrator, and an advocate who got each child set up with a therapist. She also sought out a number of organizations and state departments to help her navigate different social services. Within four months, though, the safe haven was stolen from the family. The Monster—who had verbally agreed to the move—started to stomp his foot and demand for visitation rights because how is he supposed to be able to assault his daughter if she's in a different state? Emma and her children were court-ordered back to Texas.

She returned because she had to, because her "choices" were Texas or a jail in Texas. Even though she would be jobless and homeless, even though she knew The Monster would abuse her daughter, even though multiple professionals made multiple reports about the horrors of this man, he continued to have unfettered access to his daughter, and Emma still had to move her family back.

Upon return, The Monster was awarded bi-weekly, forty-eight-hour unsupervised visitations with his daughter.

But how is that possible? Why would that happen?

Simple: A judge insisted Emma was still lying about the sexual abuse and refused to hear or acknowledge any new evidence.

In his article about the court system's mistreatment of protective mothers, Barry Goldstein says that, "courts disbelieve 94 percent of child sexual abuse reports. . . . This means in a majority of domestic violence custody cases the courts are sending children to live with dangerous abusers and rapists."

Esther became part of the 94 percent.

᪐

It's a weekend when Esther gets to stay home with her mom and siblings. She's lying on the long cushion that sits on the windowsill in Gauge, a yarn store in Austin. Esther's a few months shy of being four years old, a few months and one day shy of making another outcry. But first: yarn. Emma's looking around. David's playing on his tablet. Hannah is doing the same. Esther lays supine on her back, holding two stuffed animals from the basket full of puppets and plush animals the yarn store has for just this reason. Mom needs some quiet time to shop in the peacefully hushed yarn store. Kids need to play.

Esther is laying down, a story mumbling out of her lips. No one really hears what she's saying because she's three and hops around topics without any logic. Plus, her tongue is still practicing the fine art of pronunciation, which can make comprehending her statements a challenge.

But she's saying something about The Monster. Something about how The Monster can't hurt her. Something about keeping The Monster happy. Even if you don't hear her, you can see how her actions explain everything.

Grasping a ladybug finger puppet around its abdomen in one little-kid hand, and the end of an octopus's tentacle in the other, Esther apparently knows what to do when you have a hole and something cylindrical. Insert mass into abyss. She does this. Now her voice turns inward a bit more as she continues to talk about The Monster, about how she knows how to put a smile on his face. Even with this obvious statement, the way that Esther plays with the puppets is exponentially more loquacious than the combined shards of her fractured sentences.

These, too, are actions that Emma not only hears, but addresses to keep her kids as safe as she can. From David's first PTSD episode in April 2015, to Esther's most recent outcry in August 2017, Emma has relentlessly acted to protect her children. She's a proactive, caring, protective mother who wants to engage with anything and anyone who will relieve her family's lives of this madness.

Therapists, psychiatrists, ER visits, rape kits, CPS reports and visits, reports filed, more outcries reported, forensics interviews, computer forensics analysts, private detectives, three lawyers, countless calls to advocacy centers, lab tests, NGOs sought out, visits to police stations, a move across the country, a move back across the country, and time time time time spent on figuring out which route will lead to her children's safety.

She has been doing this for the past two years.

Yet Esther is forced to see The Monster every two weeks.

And every two weeks The Monster forces himself upon Esther.

After all of these actions and outcries, how is it that this situation persists, that a four-year-old is forced into unsupervised visits with the man who she is currently and consistently making outcries about, and how every time she has to go she screams and screams that she doesn't want to?

Because no one wants to hear about something so atrocious, let alone believe it. And God forbid somebody do anything about it.

"For decades," Goldstein writes, "protective mothers have been complaining that family courts are tilted to favor abusive fathers and that they face corruption. Court officials have tended to respond defensively and dismissed the domestic violence victims as disgruntled litigants."

Which is to say that there is another perspective on the matter of the protective mother. She's not an advocate, but a vindictive lunatic.

"All of law enforcement doesn't believe anything that I'm saying," Emma explains. "Wood County said that it doesn't make sense that my daughter would say one thing happened to her one day, and then say something different the next day. That's not because she's lying. It's because she's four years old. And, most likely, she's talking about multiple events. She's not lying, she's describing experiences—plural. Plus, she's too young to know time. Everything to her is yesterday."

But Esther's bruises on her leg, the dark purple-greens that are the perfect shape of an adult hand, are easy enough to see. The green-yellow, sticky substance that can only be described as semen that discharged from this three-year-old's vagina and into her diaper is easy enough to see, too. These are the signs of abuse that no one is listening to.

The body keeps records of these moments, these incidents of stolen innocence.

The therapist who has worked most with the kids can testify to the abuse they endure. She can tell you how you can't coach a child into playing at PTSD. You can't teach a kid how to get that look in his eyes that says he's gone. A trigger leading to dissociation. You can't teach a child how to act like he's having a flashback. You just can't teach that type of terror.

Goldstein reports that, "evaluators, judges and lawyers without the specific training in domestic violence they need, tend to focus on the myth that mothers frequently make false reports. This is not based on valid research, but rather the stereotype of the woman scorned or the angry woman." What this means, is that our society needs specific training to listen to (and, if we're lucky, validate) what a woman has to say.

Here's the flow of logic: Children are to be seen, not heard. A woman's place is in the home. And now that we're keeping it all in the family, silence has started to strangle the truth.

Society doesn't want to see the truths that mothers speak because no one wants to hear about how in more than 90 percent of child sexual abuse cases, the perpetrators are family members or people close to the family. Because if we ignore what's being said, then we don't have to face what's being done. The court is dead-set on protecting a father's right to his child, regardless that no child can defend herself at age four, nor does she know how to call 911. And this isn't even to mention what happens when the child doesn't want to go, what happens when those who don't want her to go have to watch her handed over to her abuser for regular visitations. The victimization of this situation ripples out, its effects terrorize the rest of the family.

All because we can't take a woman's word for it.

The results: inadequate services, missed opportunities, evidence just sitting there untouched, more lies than facts, and an incredible lack of follow-up. None of this is helpful. All of this is because we dismiss a mother's distress. Goldstein explains that, "The courts were routinely treating mothers as if they were not credible but . . . scientific findings [support] other research that found protective mothers rarely make deliberate false complaints." With stereotypes and sexist judgements against them, a mother can never do anything right.

"Anyway I react," Emma says, "is going to be wrong. If I sob, I'm called hysterical and uncooperative. If I stay cool, I'm suspected of lying because I'm not showing any emotion. I can't do anything right."

Yet she keeps fighting for her children's right for safety.

A mother's work is never done.

Note: Over two years later and David's story has yet to change. Each detail remains the same.

Note: Esther makes new outcries after she returns from every unsupervised visit with The Monster.

From all of this, questions, of course, emerge. Why does a three-year-old not have an intact hymen? Why would Emma put her kids through hell, lose her job, live in impoverished conditions and even go so far as to rape her own children—as one detective claimed—just for a little bit of money? Why are people willing to believe that a mother would rape her own children for money and not believe that a man is a pedophile when, as Goldstein explains, "several studies established that mothers involved in contested custody make false reports less than 2 percent of the time."

There's a high cost for the court system being wrong 98 percent of the time.

Emma knows this, has twenty-six months' worth of first-hand experience.

The high cost for the court system being wrong in Emma's experience, as of this writing:

- Therapy for three children because of how one man touched them and is still touching one of them: **$6,000**
- Legal matters to gain full custody and restrict The Monster's access to the child he is sexually abusing: **$30,000**
- Moving to a different state to keep children safe from The Monster, then moving back because The Monster gets a court order saying so: **$3,000**
- New computer to replace the one sitting in an investigator's office somewhere, one that hasn't been touched in the eight months that it's been there and that contains evidence of child sexual abuse and child pornography: **$2,000**
- Therapy dog for the children to alleviate PTSD symptoms (Note: the dog had to be left behind when the family was court-ordered back to Texas): **$2,000**
- Lost furniture and clothing and household goods and toys due to the two moves across the country and the

children's destructive behaviors when experiencing flashbacks: **$10,000**

- Flights for court hearings and unsupervised visits for The Monster: **$4,000**
- Lost wages and career advancement opportunities when Emma was forced to quit her job and move back to Texas: **$35,000 (minimum)**
- Medical: **$5,000**
- Travel costs for therapy and psychiatry as well as time off from work: **God only knows**
- Hiring private investigators, getting lab tests done, etc.: **$4,000 and then some**

Minimum total cost and counting: **$101,000**

Being vindictive sure is costly.

෧෭

When will this insanity end? When will the victims stop being victimized again and again? And at what cost? Not just financial, but spiritual, too.

"People constantly questioning my kids doesn't change their story, but it has changed the way they interact with people," Emma explains. "David still has to tell people over and over again what happened—even today, three years later. By now, he has said it all so many times that he's just kind of numb to it. One CPS worker even commented that she found it disturbing that the kids could talk about it like they talk about playing on the playground."

Now, as The Monster still has rights, Emma has discovered that her life is structured around a fourteen-day cycle. How every fourteen days Esther is subjected to spend forty-eight hours alone with her abuser.

Esther leaves. Forty-eight hours later, Esther returns with a new story or bruise or outcry or complete silence.

Set the clock. Twelve days to go. Twelve days to find evidence or talk to the right person in the right department with the right experience and right connections that will help Esther to stay home—hopefully forever.

If not, then begin the forty-eight-hour countdown.

Every other Sunday, Esther returns home with more stories to tell. Such as one about a knife. How The Monster pressed it against her vagina. When Emma hears this, she reports it to the detective the next day. Here's what the detective had to say: "Well she said he had his clothes on and it only happened once."

Here's what Emma had to say: "I don't care. It shouldn't have happened at all."

Which is true.

Esther's burden, her trauma now clearly seen and clearly heard.

That was a month ago. And still, every twelve days Esther is forced to go, regardless of what she screams about, sobs over.

"We don't listen to child victims or how they have tried to overcome abuse because we don't listen to children," David Wilson says. "Not only do we think they should be 'seen and not heard,' but they are also increasingly disliked, scapegoated and hated by an adult world that has turned young people into the human equivalent of dangerous dogs."

It's a world that has put these young people in the grasp of dangerous hands and the violence of silence. Because, really, we shouldn't have to wait for a boy to fling a puppy just so he can be heard.

The names of the children in this article have been changed for their protection.

Sources:

David Wilson, "Seen and Not Heard," *The Guardian*, January 12, 2004.

Barry Goldstein, "Widely Anticipated Article Confirms Court Mistreatment of Protective Mothers." Stop Abuse Campaign, July 19, 2017.

At a Loss

When a nineteen-year-old woman climbs five flights of stairs in a parking garage, carrying a cell phone and a plan to jump. When her best friend calls and instructs her to climb back over the railing to safety. When the woman changes her mind right then, right there on the edge of the ledge, as she agrees, as she concedes with her best friend's directions, you say, "Oh god. *Thank you.*" And when that nineteen-year-old woman slips as she tries to swing her body up and over the railing to safety, when she falls down all five stories anyway, you say, "Oh god. *Please. No.*"

But what do you say to the dead girl's best friend—the young woman who kept her on the phone, kept her on the ledge, who convinced her not to jump? Yes, what can you say to this woman who will forever blame herself because if she hadn't made her now-dead friend stay on the phone, then the woman wouldn't have lost her grip and slipped? What to say when you see what the security cameras have to say, their story of how she ran up to her best friend's body just seconds after it crashed and cracked?

What to say about what doesn't make sense?

About a life-saving decision that ended in death. About the friend who saved the woman's life, but didn't. About how she will have to live with the ghastly image of her fallen friend embedded deep within, haunting her forever. About how she will never again celebrate her own life because the night she found her best friend's body on the ground, was the night before her nineteenth birthday.

And what can you say when you see her in the morning, when you hug her tight in hopes of helping her hold some of this impossible grief, of quieting her cries that cast her body into convulsions? When you stand there, arms enveloping an unstoppable quaking, when you swallow your own sobs to stay strong, when you are certain your voice won't fissure when you finally speak, what can you say?

Happy birthday?

Which is Another Way of Saying Decay

When I opened wide—no, not even wide, just a little bit. Just barely.

When I opened my mouth just a little bit, just barely, proof of a crumbling infrastructure tumbled out, and the stench of failure filled the car so quickly, so fiercely, that windows were rolled down within seconds. And not just a little bit, not just barely, but windows rushed down, yawping, unlike me, unlike how I couldn't open my mouth because the infection inside it was so severe, so vicious that my jaw was swollen shut.

Decay

1. (of organic matter) rot or decompose through the action of bacteria and fungi
2. (of a building or area) fall into disrepair
3. undergo a gradual decrease
4. decline in quality, power, or vigor

Which is another way of saying:

1. Decay: (of organic matter) rot or decompose through the action of bacteria and fungi

Regardless that I live in a large apartment complex in an area where the actual earth—its soil—is a long-forgotten, mythical element in this wasteland of concrete and asphalt, regardless that I live on the third floor, and how there is a lack of a lake or swamp or any standing-still body of water anywhere near here—even the manmade pond became so stagnant that it surrendered its wetness to evaporation—when I sat on my balcony and smelled the disgusting, offensive stench, I stopped writing and looked around because I was certain there was a dead snake rotting somewhere near my feet. But no. No rotting reptile found. I then checked the bottom of my shoe for dog shit even though I don't have a dog and had yet to venture outside my apartment that day.

Nope.

"What in the hell is that smell?" I said out loud to myself, still trying to identify the odiferous source. It wasn't until I spoke those words out loud that I realized the stench was coming from my mouth. Soon, I would experience what septic shock feels like as it ripped through my body. Shortly afterwards, I would be puking and shaking and calling 911 and hyperventilating and my hands would turn blue and my lower back would clench and I'd go to the ER and be told that nothing was wrong. Stomach ache, perhaps. A week later, a friend of a friend who is an oral surgeon would tell me I was lucky the infection from my abscessed tooth didn't spread to my heart. A tooth infection can be fatal.

Although we're not living in London in the 1600s when the fifth leading cause of death was a tooth infection, and while modern medicine has reduced the number of tooth infection fatalities to under one hundred per decade, the fact that people die from an abscessed tooth is in and of itself harrowing.

The twelve-year-old boy who died in 2007 when bacteria from an abscessed tooth infected his brain. The twenty-four-year-old man who, in 2009, couldn't afford to get a tooth extraction or antibiotics (the total cost of which would be around $100) died from the infection. Or those like me who are one of the 830,000+ people per year who have to go to the emergency room because of an aching tooth infection. That's 830,000 people who eventually received a costly hospital bill because there isn't such a thing as emergency dental care in this country, even for something as basic as an extraction—for something that is arguably one of the easiest life-saving and preventative procedures that, on average, takes less than thirty minutes to perform.

Which is another way of saying that, at thirty-four years old, my husband almost became a widower because I don't have access to dental care.

2. Decay: (of a building or area) fall into disrepair

A bridge. A crumbling infrastructure. Concrete and metal getting tired, wearing down. Assessments are made and turned into reports that will go ignored or most likely unread, because who has the time or the money to fix something that already exists when we are trying to build more buildings and offices and highways that help to get people to work? Also, old infrastructure ignored because of the hope that more construction creates more jobs and an increase in employment means an increase in money for the city. We delude ourselves that concrete and metal are for forever, that what looks strong from a distance will always exist, regardless. Ignore the close-up, the in-your-face warning signs. We don't have the time. We don't have the money. Bridge repairs aren't our top priority. It's a bridge. It will be fine.

It wasn't.

August 1, 2007.

6:05 p.m.

Minneapolis, Minnesota.

The I-35W bridge collapsed. A 336-meter stretch of concrete, metal, and asphalt—the central and adjoining spans, and the trusses and deck—all dropped 114 feet down into the Mississippi River, crashing throngs of commuters stuck in rush hour traffic into the water below. Thirteen people were killed, 145 were injured. Note: A 2001 evaluation of the bridge reported preliminary signs of fatigue on the steel truss section under the roadway. Six years after the evaluation, six years of being ignored, the fatigue was too much to bear. Such decay. Such corrosion. The bridge buckled, collapsed.

3. Decay: undergo a gradual decrease

"... *17, buccal; 18, buccal; 19, decay. 20, buccal...*"

The dentist roll calls my rotting teeth, turning them into a litany.

Aside from brushing every day, it'd been a decade since my teeth last had a cleaning. Having no health insurance, it isn't until my aunt offers to pay $700 for extracting my cracked tooth and cleaning the rest that I go to the dentist for the first time in ten years. And when the dentist inventories my mouth, when she peeks into what she's going to have to figure out how to fix and save, when ... *17, buccal; 18, buccal; 19, decay. 20, buccal* ... I start steaming in the chair with thoughts about how this country forces us to pay exorbitant amounts of money for basic care.

Because in this country, you have to have enough money to afford good health. If you don't have the right job that provides the right benefits (the "benefits" of HSAs and HMOs and in-network and out-of-network and PPOs and limited open enrollment periods and unreachable deductibles and three tiers of prescribed medications and all the lingo of the health insurance no one really understands except that it dictates which medical professionals you can go to), or even if you have the right job that provides the right benefits, most likely the health insurance plans are too expensive to be an actual option. For example: health insurance that makes you pay $3,000 out-of-pocket for your deductible—that's $3,000 you have to pay before your benefits even begin. This shouldn't even be considered an option—not even just a bit, not barely.

The day after I was released from the ER because of that fierce, septic infection in my mouth and jaw, I went to the free dental clinic to have the abscessed tooth removed, which they mostly did, but the dentist forgot (or did she even know in the first place?) to write me a prescription for antibiotics. Thirty-eight hours later I went back in the ER with my jaw swollen shut. Again. This time, I would get antibiotics, though I could only afford the cheaper kind which ended up not being strong enough to kill the infection because inadequate meds is one of the few alternatives you have if you don't have dental insurance.

Alternatives:

- The free clinic that is only free if you have a financial planning appointment within a month of your visit, but the first appointment available is in two months and so the free clinic will not be free.

- The free clinic that costs just a little bit more than free, except during their walk-in hours which are from 8:00 a.m.–12:00 p.m. on Mondays, and don't forget it's first come, first serve, and that the waiting line winds around the building every Monday. There is no guarantee that you'll see a dentist that day. You just have to wait.

- The affordable community clinic that extracts teeth and doesn't prescribe antibiotics, that doesn't actually extract the entire tooth, that doesn't give you anything for the pain when you have a dry socket, that tells you it's your fault that you have a dry socket, that packs the dry socket for you but that refuses to do it again when that chunk of whatever it was falls out of your mouth within an hour when it was supposed to stay put for seven days, the clinic that is now demanding that you pay for those two follow-up visits even though the reason you had to follow-up was because of an inept dentist.

Which is another way of saying that because of a decaying healthcare system, I had to succumb to the free dental clinic where I absolutely received my money's worth.

4. Decay: decline in quality, power, or vigor

The bridge's aftermath: The collapse was officially declared a disaster seven days later. After the government helped and the donations came in, after the cost of just the emergency response totaled $8,000,000, it was thirteen months and $234,000,000 later that a bridge that never should have collapsed to begin with, was rebuilt. The atrophy of society lies in part in our habits—we must re-build when we don't attend to the simple issues and catastrophe strikes. Our tunnel vision means not attending to the warning signs and our problems end up costing more than millions—it cost lives, too.

The I-35W Bridge Remembrance Garden opened on August 1, 2011. Four years after the collapse, the memorial was built, its view looking right at what used to be right there, right where thirteen people died because of inept decision makers. It was a glowing result of a community coming together in the face of such tragedy. There was a focus on symbolism. On remembering.

Thirteen columns erected, a litany of names read and thirteen doves released at the opening ceremony to commemorate the lives that went down with the bridge. Money can't bring everything back after such collapse.

Which is another way of saying that the bridge finally received attention, just thirteen deaths and 145 injuries too late.

Which Is Another Way of Saying Decay

What in the hell is that smell?

It's not my mouth this time, but the gradual decay of a society that insists we all have access to the resources we need to stay healthy. And I don't have enough vigor or power to help create something else. I'm too busy, dizzy, nauseous from navigating the alternatives to do anything about the crumbling infrastructure of this society. Of my mouth.

We delude ourselves into thinking that our system is for

forever. Ignore the warning signs. We don't have time. Too busy standing in line and hoping to get affordable help, too busy working for too little, too busy sobbing from pain and praying that some other patient won't show up, praying that someone else is too busy to attend to her own health, just so there's an open appointment and an opportunity for an inadequate dentist to mostly extract only the visible part of the problem. The surface-level dilemma. A cracked tooth, an infection under its root.

All of this is a matter of ignorance. Of ignoring. We don't want to deal with what feels like a minor inconvenience.

Consider the infection, then consider what would need to be done for its eviction. The dentist and antibiotics. Healthy mouth and gums I can't afford. Now ignore. Ignore the pain as much as possible. Try to forget it's there. The throbbing is a constant reminder, but there isn't any time or money available to remove it. Perhaps the infection will tire out and vacate the mouth.

But decay won't fix itself.

Bridges won't do their own repairs.

There's another infection going on, running deep through our social foundations. The symptoms compose a long list: How our resources are spread too thin to be able to truly attend to a bridge. The threatening cracks that spread when ignored. That eventually fissured. The superficial issues we didn't listen to.

Which is another way of saying that the real issue is rooted too deep to extract, too problematic to treat.

What we think and assume versus what we actually do.

Get weary of the gradual decrease.

Brace yourself.
Wait for the buckle.
Collapse.

It Was Just a Lamp

Yeah, he threw a lamp across the room, but I was outside on the balcony so all I knew of the incident was the sound of a huge *thunk*. I heard the huge lamp *thunk*—not crash nor shatter, mind you, because the lamp was big and heavy. It had girth. Neither my husband nor I liked the lamp—its mammoth orb of a putty-colored body with a shade that defined *fugly* better than Merriam-Webster could ever attempt to do—but we got it for free from the family whose house we went to after we moved to pick up their old mattress and box spring. Fifty dollars for both. Go Craigslist. The lamp was an extra bonus even though it felt more like a burden than a gift.

That big fugly lamp was what my husband chucked across the room that morning, although I didn't actually witness the altercation so for all I know he drop-kicked it, the image of which is actually kind of amusing. Either way, I'm sure he had his reasons for the lamp-chucking. I suspect it had something to do with his untreated mental illness and semi-psychotic state of late.

But whatever. It was just a lamp. A free one, at that.

I, too, have some anger issues. I've been known to chuck a pen or two across the room when my writing just wasn't behaving. Though there was that one time when I threw the flat screen monitor on the floor because I was in a more-than-semi-psychotic state. Surprisingly, it didn't break. Though neither did my psychotic state. So off to the psych ward I went. Three days and one new prescribed medication later, everything went back to being okay-ish except for the marriage.

The trip to the mental hospital was all about emotional pain. Nine months later, I would go to a different hospital, in a different state, and I would go not because of emotional pain, but because of a physical one. An abscessed tooth, specifically.

Neither my husband nor I have dental insurance because who has ever heard of being able to take care of your body in this society without going into a suicide-inspiring debt? Ergo, ER. There, I got me some supersized ibuprofen that worked about as effectively as stopping a hurricane with a ceiling fan. Also at the ER, I was told to go see a dentist about the situation going on in my mouth. No shit. They gave me information about the free clinic in town. I would eventually find out that the free dental clinic really isn't free and that no one there seemed to know how to practice the art of dentistry.

The "dentist" at the "free" clinic "pulled" my tooth. Sort of. I would find shards sprouting up from its ground zero twice within the next year. Two days after the kinda-sorta-but-not-quite "extraction," I went back to the clinic because I got me a nifty dry socket. Plus, the infection was worse than when I initially went in just a few days prior. Oh, right. Antibiotics. They forgot to give those to me. Whoopsies. The medicinal patch they put over the festering desiccated hole in my jaw fell out within an hour. I went back a third time in three days because I was dying of pain but the dentist told me she didn't want to do anything else for it because sometimes it's better not to fuck with a hot mess. More or less.

Which, at times, also feels true for my marriage.

Aside from the horrible pain and hideous stench, another side effect of a dry socket is insomnia.

A side effect of insomnia is an annoyed husband.

Getting up every thirty minutes to ice and pace wasn't the most restful of actions, so in all of my not-wanting-to-piss-off-my-husband wisdom, I decided to try to sleep on the loveseat in the living room because I like to think of myself as a kind and considerate human being, regardless of my destructive tendencies to throw writing utensils and electronics when I'm feeling super-duper-psychotic, and even when I want to rip off my own head because of the pain, I feel like I'm still an attentive human being to other people's needs—though apparently not always. Take that night, for instance.

But first, *holy hell*, I actually fell asleep! The only way I knew that I fell asleep was because I woke up. I woke up to the sound of my husband eating kettle chips. They were crunchy and loud and at 4:00 a.m. they woke me up because the kitchen was just a few feet away from the loveseat on which my dry-socketed throbbing head not-rested.

Yeah, I was pissed that he woke me up, but I was even more irked by the riotous sound of his teeth hard at work. *Crunch crunch.* It amplified the *throb throb* in my jaw. *Oh. Hell. No.*

And yes, I then started screaming at my husband and no one likes to be screamed at when it's 4:00 a.m., but also no one with a hellacious dry socket likes being inadvertently chomp-chomped awake at when it's 4:00 a.m. Thus, I screamed.

My husband screamed back at me.

This had been our mode of communication lately.

And then the screaming colloquy took quite the turn, one

that is as sharp as that street in my town that's called Dead Man's Curve for a reason, because the topic of the 4:00 a.m. showdown somehow whiplashed from late-night snacking to all of the money my family had and he wanted. It had something to do with dental care. His teeth were decaying, too.

But tooth pain, man. Tooth pain. Mine specifically. Let's stay focused on what's important here—me. My pain. Set go.

After a good number of rounds of not-so-good verbal treatment, my husband stormed off to the bedroom, mid-excellent point I was making from the loveseat. The amount of which this exit strategy pissed me off was equal to the amount of pissed off I was when the kettle chip crunching thing happened a few thrown obscenities ago. I got up from the loveseat because, why not? I was awake. Might as well deal with this BS and so I stomped my sleep-deprived body and throbbing jaw into the bedroom and I sat at the edge of the bed, right at the feet of my husband who was just trying to get to sleep. I refused to move because I was in pain, though really it was because I can just be a stubborn bitch like that sometimes, my considerate human being qualities completely vacating me, giving room for grudges to gurgle up and join forces with my relentless shrieking.

It was a fairly quick interaction.

Husband: Go away! I want to sleep!

Me: You woke me up and then started yelling at me so why can't I disrupt your sleep to yell at you?

Husband: Leave me the fuck alone!

Me: No. You started this conversation, let's finish it. What in the fuck problem do you have with my family?

Husband: [kicks me]

My husband kicked me, which made me wobble on the edge of the bed a bit and when I regained my balance I considered lunging at him, but before I could, he decided to make sure his point was clear because he's always been a very thorough dude when it comes to be being an asshat—just like me and my bitch thing (we all have our signature traits)—he again thrusted his foot into my stomach. I fully fell back, my lunging plan foiled, and then I cried because I was about to throw up and all I could think about was how much that would *fucking hurt* what with the dry socket and whatnot.

Which is when that metaphorical light flipped on inside me. Crawling on hands and knees into the living room, stomach hurting both inside and out, I spilled myself into a huge deluge of sobs, though this specific weeping wasn't sprouting up from the physical pain—rather the emotional one—as I realized that now there would have to be exhausting relationship-talking and space-giving and using your I-statements-ing and trust-building and boundary-setting and other people's opinionating and safety-defining and deciding what's worth it and what's not worth it and my god how many couple's counseling sessions are we going to have to have because now my husband has kicked me and because, yes, now we have to fuck with this hot mess of a marriage.

And That's How You Do It

When she saw it wasn't her mom who came into the house from the garage but Samantha, Lacy stopped her giddy gallop of sorts towards the door and said flatly, "Oh. It's you."

Samantha got mad, which is another way of saying that her feelings were hurt, which can be a hard feeling to express, so Samantha got mad. Really, though, Lacy was simply, innocently assuming it was her mom who came inside, not her mom's partner. Lacy is seven, by the way. Samantha, thirty-four.

Samantha turned around and stormed back into the garage, obviously irate as all hell. Kim and I hiatus-ed our conversation, or perhaps it was more like we were voluntold to halt it by Samantha's demanding anger and its accompanying one-way, quite loud dialogue:

"Fuck this."

And

"Fuck that."

And

"I won't stand for this shit!"

And

"She hurt my feelings."

"Let it go," my friend said. "She's *seven* and probably thought I had come inside. I'm sure she just had something she wanted to show me."

"No, fuck that. That shit's rude."

"She didn't mean anything by it."

"I don't care, that's rude. Fuck her."

(And so on.)

"*And* she needs to apologize to me," Samantha said around minute six of the tiff.

"You want me to make a seven-year-old feel really upset and all guilty by making her apologize for something she unintentionally did and that *you* are overreacting to?" Kim was rightfully pissed by this point.

"Yeah. She needs to apologize for how rude that shit was."

"SHE'S SEVEN. So, what, you just want me to bring her out here so you can yell at her and hurt *her* feelings because *you're* being the child?!?"

"I don't care about her fucking feelings. She was rude."

"Fine." Eyes somersaulting out of their sockets, Kim stood up, marched inside and returned with Lacy in her wake, walking close behind, her little kid balled-up fists rubbing her eyes and practically gouging them out because that's what she does when she cries. Lacy walked up to Samantha and said sorry, her hands then at her sides, sorry she hurt Samantha's feelings, so sorry, she didn't mean to. Sorry. An overflow of little Lacy tears let loose.

"Aww Lacy, sweetie. Come here, girl—I didn't mean to make you cry." Lacy took a step toward Samantha, tentatively, because taking a step closer to someone who has been screaming at you can be a scary thing to do, and so Lacy took a step toward Samantha, tentatively. She brought her tears with her. "Oh sweetie," Samantha said again, reaching out to hug Lacy in an effort to dam up her tsunami. "I don't want you to cry.

You're going to make me cry. Don't cry, sweetie. I'm not mad anymore. We're all good, honey."

Then they hugged it out.

Samantha was okay. Lacy seemed kinda-sorta okay, and as Kim walked past me to go back into the house with her daughter, she looked at me and quickly, quietly snapped, "And *that's* how you do it."

There are subtle ways to say *fuck you*. In fact, there are incidents where a tacit *fuck you* is the only feasible response. Most of these are in the context of break-ups or marital spats. I've heard of one tacit *fuck you* that came in the shape of a woman taking all of the silverware with her when she moved out, leaving her ex only two utensils: the large, wooden salad-tossing fork and spoon.

There's the cat box I never cleaned out and the abandoned, mold-collecting dishes in the sink when I left a four-year relationship that should have ended three-and-a-half years prior.

There's the box full of ripped-up pictures my ex left sitting in the middle of the living room floor in response to my fuck-you-induced uncleanliness.

I responded by taking out all of the silver coins in our change jar, leaving her with only the pennies.

Made sense.

A friend's husband left her the entire house, but took the refrigerator.

Note: the tacit fuck you is not restricted to failed relationships. Last week, in response to one of my writer-clients who had exquisitely pissed me off with her goiter-sized ego that glared so strikingly in the email after email after email that she sent me in which she insisted my edits were wrong all over the place, I purposefully misspelled her name in my reply.

What a difference one *e* can make.

So tacit.

So, fuck you.

Because that's how you do it.

Here's something that seems totally random and in no way related to what I'm talking about: I know there isn't anything inherently gross about fingernails, but I seriously get all *uuullllllggg-ish* and *eeewwwweee-y* when my husband cuts his nails in the car. Or on the bed. Or on the couch. He's been doing this for five years.

Yick! Like, five years' worth of accumulated *yicks*.

Say, here's an idea: How about you clip your fingernails over the trashcan in the bathroom so I don't have to look at them or step on them or sit down on the cracked and dirty half-moons that used to be a part of your body?

You know, that could be one way of doing it.

A tacit fuck you was not found in the place where his foot struck my stomach. Twice. It was a pretty clear message—his sole painfully shattering something in my soul, and how I stumbled back into a heap of sobs on the living room floor because I didn't know how else to respond, didn't know what else to do.

My second girlfriend and I never directly broke up, rather we allowed geography to cut us off after we sluggishly slinked away from one another during the last year of our year-and-a-half relationship. (Apparently in my twenties my ability to love someone had a six-month shelf life.) We lacked the initiative to actually break up because by that point neither of us really cared that much—something that could have been a side effect of how we were always stoned together. She left me in Texas and moved to Colorado to pursue a creative writing degree. Right before she left, she informed me that she wouldn't need me to help her move after all because her drug dealer was going to do that for her. When she got to Colorado, she further informed me that she was dating her drug dealer and that he had moved in with her.

Score?

I wasn't terribly upset about our passive break-up but felt like I should have been, so I got drunk and dramatic and forced myself to cry to Ani Difranco's "Dilate" time after time after time. I even wrote down all the lyrics and mailed them to my not-girlfriend. She said the gesture was pathetic, that I should use my own words to express my feelings.

Whatever.

She can fuck off because that's how I did it.

One weekend in college, I went to a huge keg party with my not-really-a-friend friend, Megan, who at some point started to piss everyone off because she wouldn't share her weed. I texted Samantha about this lack of puff-puff-passing because I was drunk and just wanted to talk shit about Megan-the-Weed-Troll, which I did.

This resulted in Samantha hauling ass over to the party where she parked her big Chevy on the front lawn, got out and marched right up to Megan and spat these words into her blazed face: "Everyone thinks you're a bitch." (True story.) Then she immediately about-faced and marched back to her truck, clambered inside and then raced right off from whence she came. Samantha's truth-delivery was not a tacit fuck you. Because there are some situations where a fuck you's tacit-ness isn't as effective as just saying something less expletive (and therefore better received), some toned-down words that are really saying, *no really, fuck you.*

Here's the power of profanity left unsaid, of subtext's glittery ability to scream *fuck you* without technically screaming it, to keep quiet the explicit fact of those four letters because sometimes that's the only effective way you can say it when it just has to be said.

Here's the section on self-inflicted tacit fuck yous:

As someone who is a professional in the fine art of batshit crazy, and who has a master's in razor-wielding, with a concentration in saying everything is fine, just fine, even when nothing is fine, just fine, my self-imposed tacit fuck yous initially came in the shape of "No." No food, for starters. (The appetizer of starvation.) Fuck you, disappointing body.

And then the bulimia settled in. Each day I said I wouldn't do it, again. Each night I did it, again. Binge. Purge. Binge. Purge. Again. Again. Eventually I felt like I needed a reminder not to do that. Needed something to scream at me to stop. Visual scolding, perhaps. I swiped promises into my skin. Swiped fuck yous into my flesh. Slices as reminders to never again binge, to never again purge. Such trickery.

Swipe: fuck you, body.

Swipe: fuck you, bulimia.

Such scars.

A tacit fuck you made with a razor-sharp razor. Yes, that's repetitive. So were the makings of those markings. Again and again I told my body, my brain, "Fuck you." Again and again I told my problems, "Fuck you."

Eighty-eight instances of again and again.

That's a lot of futile reminders.

And that's how you carve out, how you confirm the presence of mental illness.

Yes.

Make scars.

That's how you do it.

My husband and I have had our intense spats, each at some point getting super ugly with the other—in my case, texting stellar shit like: "Welcome to you divorce." During one of our ugly blowouts—one that pushed me to go crashing on Kim's couch just to get away from my marriage for a few days—I had returned to our apartment to gather books and clothes, and when I was there, a thought occurred to me: steal all of those nail clippers he obsessively uses inside. Taking them would have been an exemplary tacit fuck you. But I just couldn't bring myself to do it.

The tacit fuck you is an acquired skill. Anyone can do it, but perfecting it to reap its maximum benefits takes practice and dedication. Determination and intelligence, too. Talent. Plus holding a grudge like a champ and keeping all of that anger bottled up until it's time.

Then watch me burst and hear me roar.

Only you won't.

That whole tacit thing.

Because that's how I do it until I don't.

Sometimes, I just have to scream it.

Sometimes, I just have to laser my best *fuck you* glare at Samantha when she gets all tantrumy because Kim forgot to get her Q-tips from the store.

Sometimes, I have to wonder if those slivers of nail-clipped moons are my husband's own tacit fuck you.

Sometimes, my tacit fuck you is found in my writing.

Like how I just did this.

I know my husband will hate this essay, will despise this written not-too-tacit fuck you because he thinks our private life should stay private. But if he didn't want the world to know that he kicked me in the stomach, then maybe he shouldn't have kicked me in the stomach.

Besides, I got his message the first time—after that initial foot-thrust to the gut. He didn't have to again, didn't have to re-deliver the message. I got it.

Also, just in case he does read this, here's something you should know, Husband: if we ever find ourselves in another one of our standard Category 5 arguments, instead of physically assaulting me, you can simply say, "Fuck you."

Yes, that will do.

Fuck you.

Because that's how I'm asking for it.

Balcony, 3:00 a.m.

Balcony, 3:00 a.m. Sitting out here at my desk because Husband protests the space my work-from-home career consumes in our small apartment. Working from home in the living room didn't work for him. Too crowded.

Solution: Turn half of our balcony into my office so that my work and writing are out of the way.

Note: When he's not working at his desk that is in our bedroom, he's at the kitchen table, books and papers strewn across one-half of its surface.

Balcony/my office, 3:00 a.m. I'm working because of course I'm working—I'm past a deadline for a magazine I write for because I have spent all of my time these past few days (and weeks) (plus months) (not to mention years) (you get the picture) (etc.) arguing with my husband. Nothing new. It's what we do, what happens when a marriage tries to hold onto something that no longer exists. Respect, for instance.

At 3:00 a.m. my husband has decided to join me in my office to continue his life-long work of finding new ways to tell me that I'm a terrible person. It's a full-time job, berating and blaming and vilifying me. Sometimes he even puts in overtime. Night shift.

At 3:00 a.m. my husband steps out onto the balcony—steps into my office—and begins to make himself abundantly clear.

He makes himself abundantly clear for an hour.

Balcony/my office/crime scene of a verbal beating, 4:00 a.m. I sit at my desk, unable to decide which of the following feels worse:

1. My husband walks into my office to yell at me while I'm working.
2. It is 3:00 a.m. when my husband walks into my office to yell at me while I'm working.
3. He accuses me of emotional abuse.
4. He declares that when I was sexually harassed by one of my co-workers for an entire year—a situation that eventually landed me in a psych ward because of my anxiety and depression that it spurred—what I was actually doing was fucking around behind his back.
5. He explains how I'm not a victim, but a fucking cunt for fucking around behind his back.
6. I am silent for the entire hour.
7. In the space between my desk and the door sits my husband who has cornered me and is scolding me and I'm too scared to get up and leave because I fear he might physically harm me if I do because he's done that before.
8. At some point he stops reprimanding me and just rants into the darkness.
9. The elevated amount my body is shaking.
10. The skill it takes to cry silently.
11. How quickly I start to dissociate.
12. He's too far gone in his rant to notice that I'm shaking, crying, dissociating.

13. Or maybe he knows and he just doesn't care.

14. Or maybe he knows and he thinks I deserve it.

15. After an hour, he stands up, exits my office, and goes back inside without saying anything else.

16. I wipe away the onslaught of tears and return to writing about soft-serve ice cream and iconic curlicues.

17. The article is two days late because I have been spending all of my time—even middle-of-the-night time—fighting with my husband about the same situation over and over and over.

18. Over and over.

19. This isn't the first time this has happened.

20. I know it won't be the last.

I reflect, feel how still I felt during the verbal assault. Unmoving. Frozen. Trapped. It was me in my office chair, staring straight into the darkness just beyond my desk light, staring straight into the darkness of our marriage until some part of me lifted and then I was looking down at me, at him, at our marriage, at his yelling and his position between me and freedom.

This is what it is like to talk with him. I bite back most of the time, but tonight, or rather morning, I turned to silence. I sat in my calm costume covering the surface layer of my skin, while inside I was shaking and fissuring and just waiting for his uncontrolled verbal violence to peter out. To end. No sudden movements or arguing, but just staying silent, staying seated when what I really wanted to do was sprint out of there. Sprint away. But that meant having to walk past him.

Again, the fear.

Over and over.

Better to just take it. Better to just play dead.

Alone on the balcony, 4:00 a.m. I get back to work while I can.

One-Hitter

I didn't know you wanted the one-hitter. We were both sober, after all. Had been for the handful of years we'd been married. Which is why it was so funny that you got the job with the dispensary. Colorado had just passed the pot-is-legal law, which opened up a job for you. Regardless that you had a master's degree in technical communication, you refused to get a better job than delivering pizzas. It was something about your upbringing. About how you always thought you didn't deserve what you worked hard for and that life was just one big unending struggle. So with your master's degree, you did pizza delivery. And when dispensaries opened up, someone had to deliver the weed from the weed warehouse to the weed stores across the state. You got the job and we laughed about how the last time you "delivered" drugs was in college. Work experience!

You enjoyed your job. From picking up the pot to delivering it to the pot stores that at times were a six-hour drive away, you barely had to interact with any humans. Perfect for your people-avoidance tendencies.

I didn't think the one-hitter was important to you. It was just a plain little glass one-hitter pipe that one of the stores gave you as a tip.

When we were packing up to move, I gave AJ the one-hitter. I'm a gift-giver and it was just sitting on the stove, and you didn't smoke pot but AJ was a stoner, so I figured you didn't need it and he would use it. "It meant something to me," you said after AJ left, the top right corner of your lip doing its twitching madly thing. Pavlov-like, my heart sped up a bit at the sight of that twitch. I knew I had done something wrong. I'm sorry I thought the one-hitter was just a one-hitter and not a symbol of I don't know what.

Being a legal drug runner made you realize you wanted to start your own delivery service, so you bought a cargo van we couldn't afford even though we already had two cars and I didn't say anything about that purchase, like how a few months later when I took you to the mental health crisis center at 2:00 a.m. because you ripped the glass top off your metal desk—eyes all textbook crazy-like, top lip twitching, me praying you would just get on medication already because your moods and paranoia were always my fault, of course, because even though I was asleep that night I had somehow pissed you off, somehow incited your rage while I slept—and I didn't say anything when you told the social worker at the mental health crisis center that you had a plan. That your plan was to go to Home Depot and get a hose and drive somewhere in your van and put it in the exhaust pipe and through the window and do it that way, and I didn't say anything about that, though I did wonder why you would use the van when it would be much quicker to do it in your little Saturn. That was when I knew for reals that you really were not right in the head—not that you ever had been—because the plan just wasn't logical.

I didn't saying anything about the lack of logic back then, but a few years later I did finally come to my senses, did finally think about the logic of our marriage and its lack, and I finally said, "I can't do this anymore" when I jumped out of your van at a stop light in Las Vegas. I was sick of watching your top right lip twitch, sick of how it quickened my heartbeat, sick of how it was always prompted by your paranoia that I was trying to pull a power move over you, like when I insisted on buying dinner that night in Vegas and you started berating me about it in the van on the way home, claiming I treated you like you were my "pet," or like when I gave AJ the one-hitter that I still don't know why it was important to you, but that doesn't matter now because when I finally realized it, finally screamed back, "I can't do this anymore" and jumped out of your van, I knew I no longer had to believe you were important to me.

Stunning

Scene—2001

Here. This spot's good. Lie down. Stretch out across Target's dirty tiled floor. Here it goes. I place my body directly in front of cash register number two. The fluorescent lights above are either turned off or about to be, so here my body rests in a low glow with its gray shadows. Lying on my stomach, I consider how best to position myself to make it look like I fainted. Adjust arms up, bend legs just a bit. My khakis and red shirt—Target employee uniform, of course—are getting dusty with the remnants of a full day's worth of foot traffic.

Left side of my face now on the floor, content with my faux-fainting position, I close my eyes and wait. I want my manager to find me—not to get out of work early, but to get her attention. I assume it will be just a few minutes more because I know she's almost done walking the floor, making sure everything's tidy and zoned and well-stocked before we all go home.

My calculation is correct.

Ivy's voice calls my name in a bit of a panic as her footsteps rush closer to my "limp" body. I won't remember the rest of this interaction clearly, but what will stay with me is the deep brown of her eyes as I "wake up" once she touches my shoulder, how my lids theatrically slowly open and see hers immediately, the sight they lock into and that what I see is so much concern. Finally.

I have her full attention.

Ivy helps me get up, plops me on a bench, calls my mom to come pick me up, and then sits with me. Sits next to me. Legs touching. Those eyes still concentrating on, still penetrating into mine.

Her solicitude feels glorious, and in this moment, something sparks. Eye contact's intensity now rising up a notch.

Fifteen years later, when I'm thirty-four years old and Ivy's forty-eight, we'll be sitting across a table from each other at Panera Bread, knitting and coffee-ing and chatting away. Then, in synchronicity, we will happen to look up from our knitting, look at one another at the same time. Her eyes. My eyes. That contact. Its intensity and how it will still, somehow, make my skin sizzle. Some sort of force will vibrate in the air between us so fiercely that my eyes will begin to ache. We will both break eye contact right then, right in that moment when it becomes too much. Later that day, I will write in my journal: *Does your skin hurt when our eyes connect?*

ॐ

Remember this date:

August 10, 2000

"Are you gay?" I finally ask Ivy. A second ago, she was my boss at Target who I had a crush on and who I suspected was either dating my other manager, Kathy (who's sitting next to Ivy and who—with the red curly mullet, strong forehead and determined thighs—is undeniably a dyke), or is at least super-close friends with her (i.e., Ivy is a perhaps a woman whose lesbian sexuality isn't an *if* but a *when* and by god Kathy better be taking on the important task of initiating that *when* and coaxing Ivy out of the closet because Ivy is way too cute and gay to stay locked up in there).

Kathy's eyebrows shoot up at my question and she cackles as Ivy, who's sitting across from me at the Formica table in the Target café, jumps up, grabs my wrist, and marches me into the clerical office. We enter the barely lit room and she sits me in a chair, then sits herself in the chair behind the big Formica desk[1] that's now sitting between us. We sit. She takes in a breath. Exhales her confession, that yes she is a lesbian, and although I won't remember much of anything else that she says during this conversation, I will remember this:

"Why am I telling you this?" Ivy questions herself out loud, elbows on the desk, forehead resting in open palms, a zest of exasperation in her voice. "You're fourteen years younger than me."

Neither of us have an answer to her question.

Neither of us ever will.

Obsession—three youthful versions of its epitome

1. Her lowercase *d*s have a snippet of a tail. An uplifting stroke of a pen at the letter's end. I'm 18 here, changing the way I write my own lowercase *d*s so they match hers. It feels awkward and burdensome even though it's just a slight lift. Nothing feels natural about this shift and yet I am determined to change the appearance of my penmanship. Why?

---

[1] Could we get a little more Formica in Target, please?

Because it links us, gives us something in common—regardless that Ivy rarely sees my handwriting, and even if she did, she probably wouldn't even notice the resemblance. But in my head, one more thing in common means we're that much closer. That we're meant to be in each other's lives. The logic of love—its lack, really—is housed in such magical thinking.

2. Arms hooked around her stomach, her back mashed up against my abdomen, my chest. Such heat. I hold onto Ivy tightly and because we're laughing and having such a blast I don't care that my ankle is smashed against something scalding hot on this four-wheeler. Although it's just a tiny point of contact—pinprick-sized—my skin sears. When we get back, I'll find a small dot of an open wound and when its scab falls off a few weeks later, I'll tape that flake into my journal because look: *proof.* That day really did happen. We really were at her family's ranch to set off Fourth of July fireworks and the next day Ivy really did take me on a jolting joy ride through the empty land on her mother's four-wheeler and my arms really did wrap themselves around her lovely form. The scab ensures this day wasn't a dream—it just felt like one.

3. This one is about piercings and birthday presents. It's about the small white jewelry box I give to Ivy on her thirty-third birthday, when I'm nineteen and she's still my manager at Target. It's about what's inside of that box, about those seven pieces of metal I have

taken out of my body—hoops through my nipples, a long bar in my tongue, a tiny hoop in my tragus, and lines of studs snaking up both ears. Ivy doesn't like piercings. Something about ruining God's work. She looks a bit baffled when I hand her the wrapped small box full of my metal-related identity, assuming I am giving her jewelry, which I am, but not in that way. I do this because I like Ivy and I want Ivy to like me, and so I do what she would like for me to do even though I don't really want to do it, and even though she doesn't ask me to, but I do it for her anyway because she's Ivy. The body decorations that I really love now extracted. This action driven by the hope that because of this present, this bowing down to her preferences, unrequested, Ivy will like me like how I like her. Though things with Ivy are not and never will be that simple.

ॐ

Answers to questions you probably have right now

1. *Who is this woman?*
   The basics are easy enough to answer. Ivy June Dryson. Current age: forty-nine. Current location: Waco, Texas. All the "about me" info is easily obtained from social media. But none of those facts—even now, nineteen years after we met—tell me who this woman is. Because the rest of her— the actual her—is a fertile ground of half-truths and buried pasts, tilled with avoidance tactics. Her surface level is

smooth. Controlled. But this woman is made of inner turmoil—relentlessly churning soil. Ask me who Ivy is and I'll
tell you about a friend, a mentor, a faux-mother, a guide, a
teenage fantasy, a crush, a heartbreak, a woman I couldn't
figure out how to live without. Ask me about Ivy and I'll tell
you about confusion, about the effects of emotional chaos.

2. *How long have you known her?*
Nineteen years, though fifteen of those were spent in silence.

3. *How did you meet her?*
Storytime!
Summer, 1999.
Ivy and Kathy are dating (no one knows this but Ivy and
Kathy) and they are both Chelsey's managers at Target when
Chelsey is in high school. At first, Chelsey hates Ivy because
she's the bitch that made Chelsey organize the baseball card
aisle even though Chelsey's shift was over. Chelsey is totally
crushed out on Kathy, but then that changes for whatever reason and Chelsey becomes obsessed with Ivy and hates Kathy
because Kathy is dating the person Chelsey loves, though no
one can figure out why Chelsey loves Ivy—Chelsey included.
She just does. A few years after having Ivy and Kathy as her
managers, Chelsey eventually evolves from being the high
school kid at their workplace to a solid friend, or perhaps
she's a pseudo-daughter, or perhaps she's just their cute baby
dyke eye candy. Perhaps it's all three. Either way, the two
adult lesbians befriend the late-teens Chelsey, along with an
unspoken, unidentifiable definition of what "friends" actually means. Eventually, Ivy changes jobs, Chelsey changes

jobs, and a year after she starts college, Chelsey is then invit-
ed to live with Ivy and Kathy for a summer because Chelsey's
house is filled with a drunk, alcoholic, recently jobless father
who Chelsey hates, and all of that makes her depressed and
incites her mental instability to swing even more all over the
place. Home is an unstable thing, so Ivy and Kathy invite
Chelsey to live in their home for the summer, which is exciting to Chelsey because her attraction to Ivy hasn't lessened
any in the past two years and so perhaps this is Chelsey's
chance to get what it is she wants: to spend more time with
Ivy. That is the simplest way to put this. It's the only straight-
forward aspect of this entire story, of Chelsey and Ivy's relationship. Time. Its meaning. How to spend it. Note: What
is done during that time spent together is where things get a
little dicey—the three dykes becoming a triad infused with
twinges of jealousy of who likes who.

4. *Why fifteen years of silence*:
Storytime continues!
Summer 2002.
For the last three weeks of the summer that Chelsey lives
with Ivy and Kathy before returning to college, Chelsey
eventually quits her job to be a writer and Kathy doesn't
like this. This is because Kathy knows Chelsey loves Ivy, but
Kathy is crushed out on Chelsey, and so Chelsey not having
a job gives Chelsey more time to be with Ivy. Not Kathy. The
pangs of jealousy and desire to be the alpha dog in some way
rising up in her all the way to the tips of her mullet, Kathy
says Chelsey has to both get a job and prove herself as a worthy housemate to continue to live with them and that she has

one week to do this. Ivy and Kathy go see a movie. Chelsey starts cleaning the stove to prove herself worthy, then says *fuck this*. She packs up her shit, writes a note composed of words she won't remember, and leaves. Then, a few hours later, there is a phone call in which Ivy screams at Chelsey and says some mean shit and then Ivy's silent treatment starts. Chelsey tries to kill herself. Twice. Post-psych ward, Ivy still gives Chelsey the silent treatment, which, even after a lot of begging (futile) and pleading (puerile) on Chelsey's part occurs, the silent treatment will go on for the next fifteen years.

5. *What mean shit did Ivy scream on the phone?*
   "You don't deserve for your life to get better."

ॐ

Scene—2002

I extract the folded-up pieces of notebook paper and a small pencil from out of my back pocket, sit down, swing my legs over the cliff's edge, and do what is practically a requirement to do in these sorts of situations: write terribly cathartic poetry.

Teenage melancholic poetry about the insufficient description of a heartache, specifically.

If only it were just my heart that ached.
That would be such a relief.
To have all this pain localized to one
fist-sized facet
of my anatomy.
But there's the fact that the heart beats.
Like the spreading contours of a bruise,

> *the heart acts similar—*
> *any pain stemming within it,*
> *from it,*
> *is beat throughout my body.*

An hour earlier, my young, nineteen-year-old body listened to her mind's suicidal thoughts and agreed to come here. To this cliff.

To Mt. Bonnell, a tall precipice in Austin where in one panoramic view you can see downtown to the left, and the 360 bridge over the Colorado River to the right.

I'm so alone and young and desperate and have climbed up the 106 stairs of 775-foot promontory to sit here in the expiring dusk. Soon, there will be stars. Soon, I'll put the pencil and paper down, but right now as I sit on the cliff, I have a teetering and only vague sense of what I'll do after I put the pencil down. Jump? Leap at my last line's end? Because moving on in life without Ivy feels harsh. Wrong. Almost like it's not even an option. I hurt Ivy. I don't deserve for my life to get better.

With such emotional chaos swirling inside me, all I can do is try to poeticize this dire life situation in between the stanzas of my heaving sobs.

The paper is hard to see. This has something to do with all the crying.

I don't jump (obviously), but I don't know why I don't jump.

I leave Mt. Bonnell. Go somewhere. Do something. Without Ivy, nothing feels worthy of remembering. Nothing noteworthy.

The next day, I tell a friend about Mt. Bonnell and my indecisive lack of plan and how my heart wasn't really in it even though I thought it was and how I sat and cried and wrote and wanted to jump but somehow didn't. That night, my friends are worrying, wondering where I am when I don't answer their text messages.

Finally, I respond: "cemetery." I'm not joking. Lying under a tree in the nearby cemetery. That's me. I feel safe—the safest I have felt since hearing Ivy's final, parting thoughts a few weeks ago about my life's worth. I lie with the dead like I belong here.

Then my friends arrive. They help me stand up, plop me into the car, call the nearest psych ward, and then drive me directly to it.

At nineteen years old, this is my life, de-Ivy-ed.

I have a journal devoted to her. Well, a few, actually—they were from way back when. Three in total. Because in high school, when Ivy and Kathy were just starting to become my friends/mentors/whatevers I really really *really* needed to talk about Ivy all all *all* of the time and my friends were sick of her name cluttering our every conversation. So I put my Ivy thoughts in my Ivy-devoted diary. I filled up a few of them.

Yes. That obsession.

I have five tattoos that remind me of her, too. Not all are directly related, but those five remind me of what was and what will never again be. Tattoos as testimony to having survived her friendship. I just now realized this—the fact of the five.

Math time.

Total number of tattoos on my body: sixteen.

Plus one cover-up.

Which makes a total of seventeen tattoos.

I meet Ivy when I'm seventeen.

By the time I'm thirty-five, 29 percent of my skin's symbolic artwork is, in some way, reminiscent of Ivy. (1) A bird I got on my foot when I lived with her that summer, (2) a tree (which [3] covers up her initials that live beneath it), (4) the number "240,"[2] and (5) some necessary "hope" on my shoulder after our second falling-out.

Now, considering the journals (3) plus the chapters in a memoir I wrote (2) and the stand-alone essays (3) I published in my essay collections (2), I would venture to say that 29 percent of my ink is about her, too.

Two kinds of ink. Both permanent.

Tattoos as mile markers for memories that consume me. Envelope me.

A homemade tattoo living on my wrist and under a tree reads: IJD.

Her initials.

Initially, I didn't consider getting a tattoo after Ivy barred me from her existence. But then I got drunk and the grieving was all-consuming, so much so that even post-psych ward I was feeling all suicidal-ish every time I imagined life without her. I couldn't. Couldn't go on. Couldn't let go. I needed a piece of her with me so as not to feel so completely empty. Or lost. Disconnected and devastated.

So, "IJD" tattoo.

---

[2] Because I know you're wondering: My favorite book, *Bluets*, has 240 sections in it and one of them has a line that helped me move beyond The Ivy, helped to calm me down, let me know that falling in love with a sociopath wasn't my fault. "We don't get to choose what or whom we love, I want to say. We just don't get to choose."—Maggie Nelson. So true.

Eventually, four years later, I plant a tree over it, hiding it. The waving, dancing branches covering a symbol of what I thought I couldn't live without. Of what I assumed I would never see again.

ð

Then:

- 15 years
- That's 180 months
- That's 720 weeks
- That's 5,475 days of silence
- Of the time between the last time I saw Ivy and the next time I see Ivy
- A lot can happen in 136,875 hours
- A father can die
- Three children can be born
- Relationships can build and marriages can crumble
- Trauma happens and joy happens
- Scars accumulate—words accumulate
- Facebook happens
- Connections are re-made and friends are added and messages are sent and a friendship begins to rise from the ashes
- Because anything and everything can happen in 8,212,500 minutes
- Except for letting go

ð

Scene—2017

A car coming down the street. Waiting expectantly in the open garage, tooling away at inking letters on a page, I sit, wonder, write, wait, wonder some more, wait some more. Sit. Just sit because I'm too distracted to write anymore. Then, a car. I think I see her. Car parks in front of the driveway. Yup. That's her.

I click my pen closed, the wondering done as Ivy walks down the driveway toward me. There's the gray that now dominates her curly brown strands I remember best from our Target years. There's me with a body lacking twenty-four pounds since we last saw each other, fifteen years ago. As Ivy walks to me, I wonder about juxtaposition, about the image of my current ass-length dreadlocks clashing with the shaved head I had when she saw me last.

Her head is looking down, but I can still see that smile of hers swipe across her face. Mine swipes next. It's unavoidable. Our bodies move to each other, closing the gap that separated our lives for over a decade.

A hug.

She's back.

In her car, three sets of eyes that mirror her own. Three kids who carry on the legacy of those severe orbs. Slightly slanted lids, much hidden behind them. Inquisitive looks. Each glance given with such genetic intensity. Six little replicas of what I could never forget.

ॐ

Scene—2017

It's fifteen years after Ivy screamed at me and I'm sitting in

Kathy's mother's RV where Ivy and her three kids are temporarily living. Through a series of *nothing more terrible than this could happen* events, in which more terrible things kept happening, Ivy ended up homeless in Texas because of a custody battle and needed somewhere to live. Before Kathy left Ivy five years ago, they did that whole in vitro thing and had two kids together, Ross and Monica (I know, I know, *seriously?!?*). Ivy kept the kids to herself after the breakup and then added another one to the bunch, courtesy of a five-month relationship with a man. Chloe was the parting gift, perhaps. Now, Chloe is four and Ross and Monica are seven and ten, respectively, and they all live in Kathy's mom's RV[3] and now Ivy and I are friends again and I'm living in the RV with them for a bit because I have recently left my husband and need somewhere to live. My relationship with Ivy is re-growing from that undefinable place it has forever been rooted in—our inexplicable attraction phoenix-ing. Revived. We're sitting and chatting as her kids are watching TV and Ivy says to me, "Oh! I have a picture of you. Hold on." Ivy walks to the bedroom as I stay sitting at the table, curious. She returns and hands me a photo that opens something in me. It's of me after a cross country race my freshman year in college. I vaguely remember giving it to her, but that's not what's opening something inside me— not the fact that I had forgotten that I had given her this picture, but it's the fact of fifteen years that grasps me. Ivy held onto that picture for fifteen years. What this tells me: She, too, never fully let go.

---

[3] FYI: The kids have no memory of Kathy being in their family. As far as they know, Kathy is just one of their mom's long-time friends.

ॐ

A Tale of Two Gigglings

1. 2000: A bag of Fritos and a can of bean dip. It was their normal lunch. Ivy and Kathy stood in the short line for my register even though there were other cashiers who didn't even have lines. But there they were, standing in mine. Ivy was closest to me and as the guest ahead of her and Kathy left, I looked at these two now-confirmed lesbians and couldn't hide my smile. Ivy smiled back at me, said: "Check me out." Then winked. My blush was unrelenting. A giggle escaped me.

2. 2017: She picks me up at my house again. Same driveway. Same car. Though she doesn't get out to meet me this time. And when I hop in the front seat, six little eyeball replicas aren't looking at me.

"Where are the kids?" I ask.

Ivy raises her eyebrows in a gesture that seems devious, if not out-right flirtatious, like a no-kids-in-tote-so-we're-alone kind of look because it's the end of May and the kids are still in—"School," Ivy simply says.

I meet her raised eyebrows and add a smile to the gesture.

She meets mine, smiles even bigger, wider, right back at me.

I try not to, but yeah, I giggle.

Our day begins.

∂♥

Scene: Sitting in her car, I glance over at her thin wrist and that's when it hits: I am in love with her again. Fifteen years later. It's the most split-second flip I've ever experienced and I'm a terribly impulsive woman. The love for her re-ignites in that moment, that obsession, and I know it's not ever going to go away. I'm not totally sure if it ever really did. But when we reach Chloe's school and Ivy puts the car in park, I see that wrist, and what this woman at one point meant to me floods back. Right at me. Into me. Slam. She gets out of the car and this is when I realize that regardless of whatever happens from this moment forward, I'm going to drown. "Here we go again," I say to myself as I watch her grab Chloe's hand and they skip together to the car, both laughing. I know she's putting on a show for me. And I love it. Here I am, hooked again.

∂♥

Fifteen years ago, Ivy insisted I learned how to knit. She sat me down next to her on the loveseat in her guestroom, the one I was using as a bed that summer. This is what I remember: Her, next to me, our bodies so close, those delicate fingers and wrists I would come to admire fifteen years later and how one afternoon we'll sit on her ten-year-old daughter's bed that is really a bunch of pillows on the floor, Ivy knitting and me typing, thighs touching and having the kind of closeness that I always wanted us to have.

I want to say that when she taught me how to knit, I remember the feel of that yarn in my hands, its soft strand and the slick wood of the needles I held in an attempt to do this craft, but the only sensation I recall is the pleasure of sitting next to her, sunlight streaming in through slats, and how amazing it felt to have her attention. To be paid attention to. To be taught. To learn how to do something she enjoyed. Another life aspect shared. The space between us receding. Within a few months I'll leave, but I will actually take with me a part of her. The brown swatch. That soft fabric she showed me so I could see the effect of a knit stitch latching on to a purl stitch—twenty rows of this. A small, soft brown square, just another bit of evidence I'll keep when I semi-let go of other things. I save this artifact, staple it into my journal to remember that yes, sometimes it's worth it to go after dreams, to strive for impossibility, regardless of an inevitable ending.

A Tale of Two Touches in 2017

1. Us. Her car. She's driving. And while she's driving, her hand keeps gently touching mine which I believe is my cue to lean in closer to her. I lean in closer to her. I wonder if her children sitting in their car seats behind us notice this, wonder if they know what the

continuous grazing of her hand on my hand means.
The meaning of my leaning in.

I don't know if they know, but I know that I don't
know. And I know that she'll never tell me the meaning of her touch. Never admit anything to me. Still.
Her too-tender touches feel infused with intention.

2. Then, kids are at school. Yarn shop time! We stand
   looking at shelves of soft, beautiful colors. She leans
   in closer to me than she needs to, again, grazing her
   forearm against mine. Like learning a new language
   I'll never be able to decipher, one that dives down,
   straight underneath my skin. My sense ignited with
   her soft touch as she offers a feel of the skein that's in
   her hands. I notice the store employee is watching us.
   I wonder if she thinks we are dating.

   I often wonder the same.

   This is driving me insane.

                    ❧

Scene—2017

This one is key. It's the scene that gives me hope. Early morning, after Ivy drops the kids off at school, we meet up for coffee. It's the first cold-ish day of fall and so I'm actually wearing
shoes that are not flip-flops. Black boots, specifically. Also: my

tightest pair of jeans, a black t-shirt with a little denim jacket over it. My dreadlocks are pulled back in a bun. It's a bit gray outside, but I have my sunglasses on anyway, which become a key aspect to this scene. The scene is that as I'm walking across the patio at the coffee shop, I see Ivy sitting at a seat that's in the window. Then, THIS: I see her eyes on my body but the sunglasses cover my own gaze that's staring right back at her. She's looking at me, wide-eyed, opened-mouth. As I strut closer to the door, a huge fucking smile erupts on her face. Then she turns her head down, her smile widening until she bites her bottom lip, trying to suppress it, shaking her head just a bit. I walk through the door and head over to her. She doesn't turn her head to look at me but says, "You're wearing boots." My assumption: she's blushing too much to face me. This is the moment in the entire history of our "friendship" that I have been waiting for—some form of confirmation that she's attracted to me. Flirting curiosity quenched. No denying it. I saw that smile. I *know* that smile. There are many times when I, too, have had to turn my head way from her so I can simmer down, de-blush, pick up my jaw, and give her a simple, "Hey you."

Later that morning she says to me: "I like your hair when it's back in a bun like that."

I say to her: "Yeah? I like it when you wear yours down."

What happens the next day: We meet up again to knit, as always. I have my hair tied back in a bun. She's wearing hers down.

It's hard not to notice and even harder not to wonder. But why should I think about a hairstyle's intention? We are, after all, "just friends."

But this time, there's more.

This time, I'm her "person." The one she talks to the most, the first person she thinks of contacting when anything happens or when she just needs to announce that her toes are cold. I'm the person she texts with so frequently that she tells me when she's going to go take a shower, so if she doesn't reply for ten or so minutes, that's why. I'm the one who receives her good night texts and then the good morning texts the second she wakes up—emoji coffee mug sent back and forth between us, something with knitting themes, too—I'm the person she asks how I slept, I'm the person who asks her how she slept, I'm the person who is always there, like a fixture.

I'm the person I've wanted to be since I was seventeen.

I'm *her* person.

ॐ

Scene—2017

Sitting next to each other and knitting, I feel like we are a pair. Not a couple, per se, but something more. A force. Souls syncing up, even though there's always an odd air between us—it's comfortable but tenuous. Complicated, though also like we're keeping a simple and powerful secret. Sitting in the car together while the two big kids play on the playground, Chloe decides to stay with us up front. "I wanna be with Mommy and Miss Chelsey." So she scoots onto the console between us and now it feels like we're the parents of this child, though also something more than that—that here is this four-year-old, her love for each of us is strong. Equal. I fall in love with this moment.

॰

We tend to forget about my IJD tattoo,[4] the one that proves how love can be nonsensical. Desperate. Embarrassing. I always fall in love with insanity. With those who know it, own it, show it. Those who display, convey, embrace it. All too well. Like me.

Like-minded people.

Ivy.

This is why we get along—a bit crazy in our own special, complementary ways. She and I. A woman who is old enough to be my mother with kids who are young enough to be my own. I wonder what we look like in public, what strangers think when they see the five of us—two adults pushing kids on swings; two adults pushing kids in shopping carts. Same-sex partners and their three kids? Or is it three generations out and about, grandma, mom, and grandkids?

Sometimes I wonder, too—wonder what we are.

This is the truth of our situation. The boundaries are all slurry lines.

I was slurry-drunk that one night fifteen years ago when the twelve-year-old kid took a safety pin and purple ink and went after the inside of my wrist to puncture Ivy's initials into my skin permanently, like I asked him to. A homemade tattoo.

It's the one we don't discuss.

Just like everything else meaningful because she doesn't like to talk about the hard stuff. Like who we are, like what makes us happy, like which moments have made her feel bliss.

"What do you think is your happiest moment in life—like,

---

[4] Or try to.

when it just felt like everything was finally coming together and nothing could be better than that moment?" I asked her over Facebook messenger. It was May 2017, a few weeks before she walked toward me down the driveway, and this conversation was when we first forayed into trying to re-friend one another fifteen years after our first, and what I figured was a permanent, unfriending.

"This conversation is making me anxious," she replied. "I need to stop talking about this."

So we stopped talking about if she has ever been truly happy.

This is the moment when I first encounter Ivy's communication style—how if she doesn't want to face what feels hard, she just won't answer the tough questions.

Our friendship becomes a series of unanswered questions.

(What do her touches, her closeness mean this time?)

ॐ

"Of course she's flirting," my sister counsels me. "When you think someone is flirting and it's been going on for a while, then of course they are flirting."

She has a good point—one that makes me grin again, bigger than one I can hide. Her point's veracity is what has always driven me crazy. The glances and the not-so-subtle stares. The leaning in too close. The word choice that feels more flirtatious than conversational. That soft smile and raised eyebrow. Fleeting, transient touches that aren't accidental.

Months after our reunion, right when we're starting to integrate one another into our separate lives, I get some guts and ask her directly, "Are we flirting or becoming friends?"

She doesn't answer the question directly, of course, doesn't claim not to be flirting with me, just that she doesn't want to be in a same-sex relationship again.

Then, months full of flirtation and then after I've re-fallen in love with Ivy even though I promised myself I wouldn't do that again, my desire for her becomes unbearable. In a moment of either clarity or stupidity, I just tell her the truth—that I'm in love with her.

Ivy replies to my text saying that she said she didn't want to be in a relationship with a woman (or anyone, actually) and that she has many deep relationships with women and that I'm the only one who seems not to understand that it's not romantic.

Later, I text about this interaction to Best Friend, who asks if any of these other women are gay.

"No," I say.

"Then she needs to consider her audience."

But, I know Ivy—she isn't ever considerate.

ఎ✷

Remember this date in Chelsey–Ivy herstory?
August 10, 2000
"Are you gay?" I had finally asked Ivy.

And now this: When Ivy's jobless and living in the RV with her three kids and just trying to manage the chaos that poverty can cause, my grandmother dies. A few days after her death I receive my $10,000 inheritance. My first thought: Ivy needs some of this. Maybe it's about me always trying to be the swooper-in-er and save the day. Maybe it's because I'm crazy in love with this woman and want her to have everything that I can give her to make her life better. Whatever it is, I decide on giving Ivy a small chunk of that money.

I sit down to write her a check and debate if I should do $2,000 or just $1,000. I decide on the smaller amount so as not to blow through all my money right away. Then when I go to write out the check, my jaw hits the fucking floor and I know I absolutely have to write the check for $2,000. Later that night, I meet Ivy and her kids at Target and hand her the check.

It's all about today's date:

August 10, 2017.

In other words, seventeen years—TO THE DAY—after I went to Target in 2000 to ask Ivy if she was gay, I'm handing her a check for $2,000 while we shop at Target with her kids who I help to take care of more often than not.

Even now I don't know what to think about this coincidence.

I just hope that it holds meaning.

And I don't know what to think about how it takes her a week to thank me for the check. Soon, though, I'll learn the consequences of pointing out her flaws, such as her lack of gratitude.

ह♥

There are no knots in knitting. The craft is too fluid, too inter-connected to knot up a part of it—something that would essentially suffocate the yarn's vibrant, continuous energy. Knitting should never be in knots, its purpose then clogged, its intuitive loops tangling up instead of labyrinth-ing around.

"You're fourteen years younger than me. Why am I telling you this?"

She called it. Started it. Stated the inexplicability of our connection when she came out to me and never anyone else, and it continued to tangle up with a bunch of *what does this mean?*s.

At first, I understood how knitting worked just about as little as I understood how my relationship with Ivy worked. I see now the larger aspects and intensified elements of what creates the fabric of our confusing connection, but when I zoom in on the particulars, the *why*s and the *how*s and the *what*s are all knotted up. It's the details that make the difference and I can't decipher any of them.

Knitting is an act of manipulation. Power, control over a thing. Take this strand in your hands and twist and turn and loop it to create a certain effect, demand for it to abide by your rules.

Take pleasure in seeing it succumb to you.

❧

I tell her: "I can't stay mad at you." I tell her: "I don't know why I can't stay mad at you." I tell her: "You piss me off, but then I see you or we talk and I just can't be mad at you."

Which is true.

But I don't need to tell her these things because she knows them. Has always seen how quickly she can de-escalate me with a soft hand on my shoulder, with some eye contact, and a spreading smile.

We both know how this works. I'm helpless here, can't resist her, can't resist doing anything and everything for her.

What this means: she uses me.

And I can't tell if I like this or despise it.

"Just be the adult and get over it," Ivy texts. "The suitcase is still in the trunk." Such a nice deflection from the question I just texted her:

"Is Monica bitchy to everyone, or am I just special?" I assume it's the latter because her rudeness and disrespect toward me always feel so direct.

Before this, late one night in the RV, Monica groaned and grumbled to her mother while standing right in front of me, "When is she leaving?" That's a genre of rudeness I had never before experienced.

Or, when I ask Monica to stop messing with the windshield wipers because she's going to break them and her mom will get super angry if she does, and then Monica does actually break them because now they won't turn off and I tell her such and she says, "You're just so stupid. They've always been like that." Then Ivy gets in the car, yells at Monica for breaking the windshield wipers. Monica glares at me.

Or, when Monica giggles at me as she admits that she lied and acted like she was scared of me to get her mom to kick me out of the RV when I was living with them. This left me homeless for ten days until my own mother financially swooped in and paid a deposit on an apartment for me.

Or, when Monica steals her mom's phone and starts texting me, teasing me and makes me think it's Ivy who's being loving to me.

Though Ivy is terrible to me. After I ask my question about Monica's targeted disrespect, after Ivy deflects by responding that Chloe's suitcase in which she planted a GPS device inside of it to monitor where Chloe goes during her court-ordered visitations with her father, she says, "Just be the adult and ignore her."

"But she'll just keep doing it," I respond.

"The suitcase is still in the trunk," she again deflects.

I wait a few hours until I bring up the Monica issue again and how not addressing it won't make her attitude change. And again, Ivy deflects with another suitcase update. A few more hours, I try to start up the issue again. Again, a luggage update.

"The suitcase hasn't moved."

"Neither has this conversation," I text back.

An Ivy explosion.

Texts full of belittling and disrespect that's worse than anything Monica could ever dish out to me. Ivy's a true professional when it comes to delivering an emotional beating. Then, after her CAPITAL LETTER STORM that's all about how I'm crazy and hyper-sensitive and immature, the texts just stop.

Silence.

For weeks.

For weeks, I plead, apologize. Nothing. No reply. I think I might die. How could I let her slip away from my life again? I got her back and then I made her go away again. Three weeks of no communication. Then Ivy feels like texting me again, says she needs me to watch the kids.

Three months later, Ivy is exasperated with Monica's disrespectful attitude toward her and gets to work screaming back at her daughter to shut her up, to gain respect through her punishment threats.

Not once do either of us bring up how I told Ivy three months prior that ignoring the behavior would only make it worse. I bite my tongue, stay silent on the matter.

આ

Scene—2002

Still sitting on the loveseat I used as a bed at Ivy's house during that summer when I lived with her, her leg was still touching mine as she sat next to me, watching me knit, observing my movements as I tried to concentrate on the yarn and the needles and my hands but my eyes kept wandering over to that spot where our legs touched. After I knit ten rows, I handed my handiwork over to Ivy. Within seconds she started frowning. There were too many stitches. She turned the swatch over in her hands, said: "You're doing something wrong." Fifteen years later, it will begin to feel like I'm always doing something wrong. Each of my extra stitches are errors I didn't think were a big deal. They're just stitches and I don't feel like undoing them for fear of fucking them up even more so just keep knitting.

But when you skip over what seems innocuous, something that's such a little thing, the domino effect of errors proceeds. How not attending to one issue will make all of the others off-course. The end result: a mess you can't bear to look at. Nor fix.

A project ripped out. Yarn looking like intestines splattered on the floor.

This is how she undoes me.

આ

Aside from giving someone the silent treatment, one of the other main signs of an emotionally manipulative relationship is when the other person makes you feel like every disagreement you have is going to be your last. This creates a trap, of course, for the victim. Don't do anything to make her angry or she'll ditch you. Don't express how you really feel, because the last time you did that she almost shut you out of her life completely, and so you're already very lucky that she took you back, so JUST DEAL. It's better to be miserable and in her life than not be a part of her life at all.

Ivy got angry at me more than a few times that year. Each time I thought I had lost her again, thought she would never accept me back. I had many reasons to believe that was true:

- When I show her text message proof of how she's making conflicting statements in a text conversation, she said: "You've crossed a line. There is nothing you can do to fix this."
- When I pull her son off of his sister because he's on top of her and punching her and she's screaming that he's hurting her, even though Ivy told me not to restrain him in any way I still grabbed him off her, she said: "You betrayed me. Things will never be the same between us again."
- When I pointed out that she needed to apologize for using her children to hurt me but she said I'm the one who created this mess by criticizing her daughter's attitude, it was this: "You have broken my trust and it will take a really long time to gain it back, if that even happens."

But then (thankfully!)[5] Ivy would "take me back" with these texts:

- "I'm a very forgiving person. I've decided it's not worth it to lose a friendship over this."
- "I'm a very forgiving person. I've decided it's not worth it to lose a friendship over this."
- "I'm a very forgiving person. I've decided it's not worth it to lose a friendship over this."[6]

Her key phrase. It was music to my tone-deaf ears. Each time she said it, my heart leapt and I promised myself I would never do something so stupid again that could possibly fracture our friendship. If I knew doing something was going to make her mad, I learned to just deal with it on my own and move forward.

I'm a very forgiving person. Though at times, like right now, I wondered if the friendship was worth it.

❧

"Man, you didn't wish me happy birthday and it sucked," I text her.

Ivy denies this (which is stupid because look at the texts—

---

[5] Hindsight sarcasm!

[6] Being a person who excavates her past to write essays, I saved all of the text-sparrings I had with Ivy. The first time I saved the compiled texts in a pdf, I titled it, "IJD final texts." But then she talked to me again. Then we fought again. Then I had to save a new pdf and call it, "IJD final texts for reals." Then, "Seriously, IJD final texts." And, "The End-All Texts of IJD Texts"

not a birthday wish in sight), then blames her children for it and still never acknowledges or gives well-wishes.

So now I'm feeling sad about the lack of celebration for the thirty-fifth anniversary of my very first accomplishment[7] and so when our nightly routine of texting back and forth until we fall asleep—always sleeping with phones in hand because texts are exchanged until one of us doesn't respond because she has dosed off—differs from the usual conversations because I'm significantly and noticeably less-energetic about her life and her new theories of how everyone has failed her, even her own children, Ivy doesn't text me a good night or a good morning the next day.

We have plans for tonight and so I stop what I'm doing about an hour prior to said plans, then head in the general direction of our meet up location—Baskin Robbins for ice cream before Chloe leaves for the bi-weekly visitation she has with her father. Ivy always texts me when they're headed to BR because children don't allow for you to name a specific time for when you will arrive, so I walk around the Target that's across the street, again waiting for that text to tell me when we're meeting up.

I always leave by 5:40 p.m. to drop off Chloe. Three children under the age of ten going into an ice cream store on a Friday afternoon, having to sample each flavor, then deciding on just *one* to eat, then choosing cone or bowl, and then sitting down and licking away all takes *at least* forty minutes.

5:02 p.m., I send her a text.

Me: Do you need me to drop Chloe off?

[7] Breathing.

When there is no reply, I realize that my uninterested attitude in the context of ALL THINGS IVY from the previous night has resulted in yet another silent treatment punishment.

Now it's 5:15 p.m.

Me: Stunning.

A minute crawls by. Then, hallelujah—a reply!

Ivy: Sorry was in BR. My dad is going. What's stunning?
  Me: Your lack of communication and consideration.
  Ivy: ?
  Me: You said I was dropping her off. I planned my night accordingly.
  Ivy: Well then you have bonus time to write or do whatever you want/need.
  Me: It doesn't work like that. If you had told me you didn't need me sooner than 15 minutes after the time I usually meet up with you guys, then okay. That's something different.

No reply.

That was Friday. By Monday afternoon, the silent treatment is still in progress and I'm livid and again find myself for the second time in my life saying *fuck this* in the context of my whatevership with Ivy and how she treats me.

So that Monday I send her a text: "I'm moving. The next time you are to contact me is to inquire about my address so you know where to send the $700 you owe me. Your car insurance is good until the twelfth. Best of luck, Ivy."

No reply—which I'm still undecided if her silence is a) a sign of respecting my boundaries, or b) Ivy just being her usual disrespectful, abusive, silent self.

And then the next day arrives and the regret arrives because pre-"fuck off"-ing Ivy, I hadn't realized that cutting her off also meant cutting off the kids. Well fuck. There is no way in hell I can walk away from the kids.

So I send her another text: "I need to walk away from you because I am not okay with how you treat me at times. I thought I could do this, but I can't walk away from the kids."

No reply.

A year goes by. More years have gone by. Still, no reply—see above for the silence's possible cause, though now I'm leaning toward option *b*.

Being friends with this woman is:

1. A tango of tenuous trust.
2. A waltz of, "What did I do wrong this time?"
3. An endless game of "Mother May I?"
4. A maze of subtext.
5. A lightning show of lies.
6. A thunderous burst of timely love-bombing.
7. An obstacle course of hopes and delusions.
8. A pop quiz on testing patience.
9. A swim through second guesses.
10. An act of survival.

꙳

She taught me a new way to cast the yarn onto needles to start knitting a thing. This is fifteen years after the last time she taught me how to cast on. The two methods are different. I don't remember the first—like how I don't remember too much of that time fifteen years ago when we stopped talking a month or so after she taught me how to cast on. I used to think knitting was a series of knots. Perhaps that was my problem. Thinking that if we got knotted and tangled, we could just undo it, could figure it out and move forward. But because knitting is actually a series of loops, if a stitch drops, everything immediately starts to unravel. Slip.

꙳

Scene—2018

The day after my birthday, a few days before I send the final fuck off text, I'm in a parking lot, in my car, and this will be the last time in my life I ever see Ivy. She's standing in front of it, guiding me as I carefully reverse out of a tight space between two cars. She guides with hubris and authority like how she has always guided and commanded me.

I don't know yet how perfect this moment will be. How this will be the last time I see Ivy and I am literally slowly backing away from her.

What Weeps

Before I stop coming, I start sobbing. This has been happening a lot lately. Tears gush before my orgasm can finish gushing through me. Out of me. I know this is about release. About grief. About how I'm alone when this happens because it's after my divorce and before the other one I love will love me back like that. She never will. And yet, I wait. Hold out hope. Hold images of her in my mind to block him out. I come and I cry and I finish coming so I can finish crying.

Alone.

Within the first four months after my divorce, I broke two vibrators. I hadn't known how sexy freedom could feel. In my marriage's absence and the subsequent release from the stress of mutual spousal mistreatment, I am now able to have four orgasms in one sitting. Frequently.

But that was before I started sobbing and climaxing. Simultaneously.

Like right now.

I flop to my side, my only company still whirring inside me. I hold it, keep it there. Steady. I hold myself as I sob. As I come. Come undone by those teenage fantasies of her that will never come to fruition and by the other ones of him that did but will never come back again.

He loves me and I love her and I don't know if I'm grieving my ex-husband or pre-grieving what I know will never be.

Either way, I have come to understand love's inequality—its imbalance.

This isn't about loneliness—but impossibility.

And not knowing how to surrender to its inherency.

June Bugs

I've been talking to June bugs lately. Each night since I've lived in this apartment that you will never actually see inside of (because I've constructed a you-less place and it needs to stay that way, and thankfully I have a friend who reminds me to do this—to start a new type of living that is not toxic with memories of you or us or our marriage and so, yes, when you blamed my friend for our downfall, you were, in a weird way, correct—but not because she tried to ruin anything between us, but because she empowered me, gave me hope and support, encouraged me to protect my heart and to move beyond your abuse. So while you might blame her, I thank her.) Anyways. The June bugs.

Each night since I've lived in this apartment that you will never actually see inside of, right before I go to bed, I sit outside my front door and write under the porch light—which, I have come to discover, is the happening place to be if you're a June bug within flying vicinity. As I write, handfuls of them dive-bomb me throughout the night, like how they're dive-bombing my head right now. *Thunk*. Oddly enough, I've become so accustomed to their company that now their diving feels like an old joke between friends, like a familiar form of playfulness.

Last night, when I was outside and was trying not to write

or think about you, I noticed a June bug was on my knee. Black and shiny, it just sat there. I looked at it for a moment, wondering how I didn't feel it *thunk* onto my knee, and then I said, "Hello." Soon after, a second June bug joined, though this one was green. I stared at my knee some more, stared at them, and said, "June bug. Party of two!" And then I laughed out loud because lately I've been feeling lonely. Those June bugs sat on my knee all night like they were keeping watch, keeping me company, keeping me to keep on writing about everything and anything but you, helping me not to fall back into those obsessive, destructive recollections of our failed marriage. In the simplest of terms, they were, well, they were there for me.

I tell you this because all of it is about more than just our imploded marriage. It's about our fourteen-year friendship that started with the more-than-friendship "friendship" with its OMG-let's-just-keep-getting-drunk-together-so-we-can-flirt aspect to it, our nine years of silence because that's what happens when life happens, and then our reconnection and then the two-month-long long-distance relationship and then our sudden marriage, and now, finally, this five-years-later flailing. It's about how I think those knee-squatting June bugs perfectly speak to what we thought we were. Two same-yet-different beings finding each other, silently sharing a space in this chaotic world, and just sitting still together. Keeping each other company. Providing comfort, perhaps. Like a partnership. This is what I love about the June bugs—their ability to just sit and exist. I feel like that's what we had early on in our marriage and it felt loving and perfect. And it's what I mourn the most— how I miss the good us, miss the calm you. Miss how we simply existed together because not doing so just didn't make sense.

I went to bed feeling tranquil, feeling that if we were meant to be together, then we will one day re-find one another and go back to that calm existence, or perhaps even create a new one.

This morning, when I went outside with my coffee and notebook, I saw a June bug corpse right outside my door. Not the green one. The shiny black one was lying on its back, body rigid, stick-like legs folded into themselves. I felt like this death should have made me sad after seeing how much life it had just the night before—how much life it gave me. But it didn't make me sad. Things die. Especially clumsy insects. When I looked at the dead June bug, what I felt wasn't a sense of failure or grief, but hope. Hope because this isn't about the comfort of silence or how to re-create a co-existence in calmness, but it's about the green June bug. How in the morning, she wasn't still sitting there. How at some point she had moved on. Flown elsewhere.

And how she kept on going, regardless.

(C)leave

In my wallet, the purple plastic heart she presented to me in her tiny fingers, handing it over as she said: "Miss Chelsey, this is for you so you know I'll always love you."

That was the last day I saw her.

Purple plastic heart held onto, I know I'll always love her too.

❧

I grab an ice cube.

I need cold to slide along my arms—a technique I was taught ten years ago in a psych ward to endure the hard moments that surged me, seized me, the ones I wanted to slice through as if that were a solution. Using this tool now—the ice cube, not the razor—I rub it along my arms, scars like sandpaper to the solid substance, scrubbing it to liquid much quicker, slicker than a smooth surface could. The ice is supposed to relieve this pain—to snap me out of this moment where a razor blade feels like something that can fix anything because everything feels broken.

A four-year-old sent me crashing to the floor.

That's not a metaphor.

Actually, it's the lack of a four-year-old that fissures me.

૨૭

An unemployed forty-nine-year-old single mother of three children all under the age of ten needs help. I was that help for my best friend. I'd known her for eighteen years, though we hadn't spoken for fifteen of them. A past fight about responsibility had thrown our friendship into a falling-out until fifteen years later when we reconnected. So our relationship was tenuous. Unpredictable. Exciting at times because of that connection that comes when it just feels right to have a certain person in your life, though also unsteady as it was brimming with past complexities. Regardless, I moved to the town where she lived to help take care of her kids—for free—as she job-searched and eventually landed a low-paying retail job.

For forty hours a week, I watched her kids after school, trying to keep a four-, seven-, and nine-year-old entertained and not killing one another. The seven- and nine-year-olds questioned why they had to do what I said because "you're not our mom." The four-year-old, though, quickly became my friend. (No—more than that. More than what a simple word could describe.) At the library, she sat on my lap for story time while her siblings bickered at the computers. I read her books, made paper crowns with her and those top hats that she called a "gentlemen's hat," and ran her to the bathroom each time I heard her little kid voice tremble, "Um. Miss Chelsey? I need you." More than a babysitter, I felt like her mother. I'd never wanted kids because I had thought I was too selfish to want to sacrifice my time and passions to properly care for a small human, and then this girl came into my life and I experienced it—that bond, that love, that I-would-die-for-you sense of protection and devotion only a mother figure can feel.

ॐ

Moving memories captured on my phone. Me, holding her, spinning her, our synchronized glee and that soft little hand resting on my chest as we twirled, her palm pressed against my heart, her body comfortable on my hip, like she belonged there.

Originally, I took this video of me and the girl to text it to her mother while she was at work. It was one of those foggy weekend midmornings when the kids were bored, mom was working, and it was my responsibility to get them outside, to expend some energy, to make sure the nine-year-old wore her helmet and to help the seven-year-old get his feet on the pedals, and to entertain the four-year-old when she got frustrated with her lack of tricycling skills.

That's when I would twirl the girl.

"Do you want to be a bumblebee or a butterfly?" I would ask, the names we came up with to call the different ways I held her small form as we spun.

"No just twirl me Miss Chelsey!" she declared on that particular morning. So I picked her up, adjusted her on my hip and we twirled and twirled, spun until our giggles meshed into one dizzying squeal.

"You guys are so dumb," the nine-year-old declared, her younger brother chiming in, "I hate how stupid they are," the stubborn animosity they had for me because I don't know why was never hidden. Still, the girl and I kept twirling until I stopped us with an idea.

"Let's take a video for your mom!"

"Yay!" the girl clapped. Adjusting her slight frame on my hip I pulled out my phone—the same phone I sob with now—put it on selfie mode, hit record. My face so close to hers.

"Wanna show mommy what we've been doing all morning?" In the video, the girl grins, then holds on tighter to my shoulders, my neck. I spin us in another circle, the girl squealing "WEEEEE!" until I stop the spinning and we look into the camera.

"Hi Mommy!" The girls says, waves.

"Hi!" I repeat. The video ends. I hit send.

I sent that video to her mother—the woman I met when I was just seventeen. She was my boss at my meaningless high school retail job, but within a few years we went from boss/worker to mentor/mentee to friends and then even to roommates for that one fateful summer before my sophomore year of college (this woman's alma mater, of course, the college she insisted I go to and so I did because I did everything she said). Our connection grew regardless of the fourteen-year age gap. But then there was a fight over how I had quit my job to spend the rest of the summer writing and she didn't like that and said I had to prove myself as a responsible human being to keep living with her, and I didn't like that so when she was out at the movies, I moved my stuff out of her house, only to then answer the phone a few hours later to be screamed at about my selfishness and my immaturity and, "You don't deserve for your life to get better!" And that was that.

Fifteen years of silence.

The first fallout was full of my suicidal thoughts and an unshakeable depression because this woman was no longer in my life, wouldn't return a text or a call or an email. Then years later Facebook happens, and I eventually reach out to her one drunk night. A friendship finally re-formed to the point where I became the one who took care of her kids while she worked, who integrated herself back into this woman's daily life, who re-became her best friend for a year until she started to manipulate me and my time, started to take more than I could give. How she wouldn't discipline the nine- and seven-year-olds when they literally told me to fuck off, how she would cancel plans without telling me, how I was her bank and her therapist and her free full-time nanny until she decided I wasn't needed anymore. Until she got laid off and started brushing me off like I didn't matter, like I didn't move to her town to help take care of her family, like I wasn't the one who taught her son how to swim and ride his bike. Like I wasn't the one who her daughter would give a purple plastic heart to, and then say, "I'll always love you."

I should have known better—I shouldn't have thought re-friending this woman was a healthy lifestyle decision, but especially I shouldn't have watched the video of me and the girl and our closeness because those were the images that sent me crashing to the floor, grasping for an ice cube as if it could save me.

ॐ

The urge to cut was not about wanting to die. It was not a cry for help, though surely I needed a lot of that six years ago after I was traumatized from being sexually assaulted. Back then, cutting was all about control, about re-taking control of my body, about harming my skin so I had something to take care of. It felt maternal, almost, attending to my wounds. I bandaged them, cleaned them, changed their dressings each day, mothered my skin back to health, protecting its vulnerability from the world. Once safe and starting to scar, I continued to need a new cut to care for. Needed a distraction—something to nurture while I avoided having to figure out how to take care of myself, how to mother this self and its trauma-filled past back to health.

੩◑

With impressive strategical thinking, my friend got me to serve her—to live near her, to take care of her kids, to give her my attention, my time, my money, my love, my care, my devotion, my everything—because she made me feel like I was serving my life's purpose by helping to keep her daughter safe. She used her kids—that four-year-old and her two siblings—to reel me in. Texted angelic pictures of the sweet girl sleeping.

And then I would question her, catch her in a lie about her plans or finances, and confront her about it, and I would instantly receive a two-week silent treatment—sometimes three. Just as quickly as she sucked me into her life, she'd bar me from it and from her little girl she knew I loved. And then she would need me again. And then I'd return again, always ecstatic to see the girl.

Each time: "Miss Chelsey! Where have you been? I missed you!"

Each time: "Oh I've just been so busy with work but I missed you so much!"

Each time: Scooping her into my arms, we twirled in circles, our giggles melding together with each turn.

ॐ

Then after one too many disagreements, one too many incidents of disrespect, one too many silent treatments, I spoke up, said *enough*. I sent texts because she hid behind her children, would never have serious conversations in person, wouldn't face any criticism about how I felt used, unappreciated, only called on when needed and not respected like the family member I felt I had become. I texted that I didn't like how she treated me at times. Essentially, I said I was *done*, that I was moving. She never texted me back. Never. A year's worth of texts and phone calls and emails full of pleading. Nothing. It's been a year now, the same amount of time that I took care of her family, her silence screaming at me about how she despises me, keeping the girl away from me. Our second falling-out means I lost more than my friend this time. I lost my little girl that was never mine to begin with.

I rebelled against her mother.
I resisted manipulation.
I stood up for myself.
Cause. ➡ Effect.
Disrespect ➡ I left.

Now, this silent treatment is permanent.
How the silence permeates me, slices me.

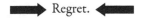 ➡ Regret. ⬅

॰॰

I'm weeping, tears mixing with melting ice. Ice to break up this moment, to take the urge to hurt and flip it to the strength to do anything but cut. This is about control. All of this is. Control of me, control over whether I get to see the child, control over if and how we can repair a friendship. Again. The sense of control over my life I feel only when I'm harming myself. No one else can touch that, can take that away from me.

॰॰

Cleave.

॰॰

Chelsey, she was just your (now ex) best friend's daughter, I tell myself. *Was just a four-year-old*. But my mind retaliates its own thoughts. Because yes, she was just four years old, but she was a four-year-old who never failed to make me laugh as she made up a song for every moment, did yoga in the shower as I bathed her, grabbed for my hand whenever we walked together, climbed into my lap every chance she got, jumped up and down and clapped and squealed my name each time she saw me, a not-my-little-girl who made me feel like my life had a purpose. To protect and mother her more than I had ever done for myself.

॰॰

Now, twelve months of silence later, her kid-laugh fading, retreating from my memory, one word and verbal tic at a time as the tide of remembrances recedes. Twelve months is one-fourth of her life. I want her in my life for a larger percentage than that. But the chance of her mother and me becoming friends again is roughly notgoingtohappen% so I need to just let go.

êð

The ice cube is somewhat working. I've gone from bawling to crying. My skin is calming down, chilling out a bit. But numb can only help so much. Ice is just a Band-Aid. I need to get to the root of the problem. I need to stop reminiscing, stop re-watching these videos of her and me and of what used to be.

I look at my arms and think of the soft, smooth flesh of this girl who was not of my flesh. I would rub lotion over her whole body after she got out of the shower and after she ran around naked because she hadn't yet learned how we women are supposed to hide our shameful bodies. Hers was the innocence I no longer possess. The flawless, scarless skin. She hadn't asked about my scars yet. Those lines that prove there was a time when I was not okay.

Like how I'm not okay without her.

Like how I'm not okay now as I wonder who is taking care of her. Who's twirling her and making treasure maps with her and celebrating whatever letter of the alphabet she learned at school that day? Who's dancing with her to make teeth brushing time more fun and reading to her those beloved rhyming Christmas books even though it's almost April? Who's putting peppermint candies in their glovebox for her because she loves those too, and expects to find them there because that's where Miss Chelsey keeps them? Who's she running toward and giving one more hug and kiss goodbye to each time they have to leave?

༄

(C)leave.

༄

I find relics of my not-daughter around my apartment, in my car. The fancy folding fan she picked as her prize with the tickets we won from the skating rink's arcade. That was the last day I saw her, the day she gave me her purple plastic I'll-always-love-you heart.

I carried her around the roller-skating rink that day, getting her accustomed to the movement before her skates touched the slick floors. How I held her, eventually becoming slippery with sweat, but she wasn't ready to let go.

"You want to try it yourself?" I asked, adjusting the girl and the added weight of her skates on my hip.

"No Miss Chelsey you have to hold me!"

"Come on girl, you can do it. I'll hold you up!"

"I'm scared Miss Chelsey," she said, tightening her full-body grip on me.

"Alrighty honey. I gotchya." Circling the rink, the girl not ever letting go of me. I can still feel her in my arms now, feel her warmth even with so much cold pressed against my skin.

This was right before Easter, and each time we took a break, she found another one of the candy-filled plastic eggs the staff had hidden throughout the building on Good Friday. She didn't keep these eggs she accidentally hunted down, but instead turned them in to lost and found, worried another kid would be sad because she had lost her eggs that lay hidden behind the trash can or sat unassumingly on a table next to the napkin dispenser. She found something special, but gave it back because she didn't see it as hers to keep.

If only this were a game of Finders Keepers. I have found the person in this world who has made me feel like I belong here, that I matter, that I can bring joy into someone's life and take care of them, and that I have so much of that life to live and love to give. I found that person in my ex-best-friend's four-year-old daughter. I found her, but I wasn't able to keep her—I hadn't considered how my rebellion against her mother would force me to give her back.

ॐ

Losers. Weepers.

ॐ

Some days, most days, I think it would be easier if the four-year-old (wait—no—she's five now) were dead. The finality of a no more. Not that I wish her dead, but it feels like it would be easier to let go of someone who no longer exists than trying to let go of someone who lives and breathes a handful of miles away from me and who didn't have a say in when Mommy made Miss Chelsey go away. So instead of reckoning with a death, I'm on the floor, trying to un-fissure myself with an ice cube on my arm because of those moving memories on my phone. I'm grieving the child I lost who is still alive and yet I'm no longer in her life. That is what hurts. The pain of missing her, the relentless tidal wave of grief. It retreats at times, then returns. It leaves. It comes back. Always. It always comes back. The real pain, though, stems from the fact that I know she won't.

☙

The ice slinks away as I sniffle myself back to breathing. I stare at the water for a little while, thankful it isn't a pool of blood. I have survived this moment without her. Without an Exacto, too. I have taken care of myself without a cut. It's been eleven years and counting since the last swipe, and I want to keep it that way. But what next? I can't see an ending to this part of my life's story like how I can't figure out how to end this essay. It's because I don't want anything related to the girl to end.

But things have already ended. The four-year-old is no longer four. She isn't that girl and in fact with each passing day, she ages further away from being that girl I loved. Even if in another fifteen years her mother and I re-re-become friends, the girl will no longer be the girl I knew, the girl I remember.

That thought is hard, though this thought is harder: In the context of a full life, one childhood year is just a glimpse of an existence. While the purple plastic heart means something to me, represents the moments with the girl that have shaped me, I must admit that it's a heart she will forget.

I am a moment she won't remember.

A Seventeen-Pound Surprise Ending

I wake up every morning surprised I'm still alive. I hate surprises. I talk to my imaginary therapist about this.

"Surprised like how?"

"Surprised like, 'Seriously God?!? You're going to make me go through another day? Fuck you, Man.'"

She asks if I have a plan. I never know how to answer this question because I can't ever tell if my fantasies can be categorized as "plans." Like, if I have considered and recognized my urge to jerk the steering wheel to the left real hard when I'm going 80 mph down I-35, wondering if the force of slamming into a concrete barrier would flip my car and crush me, is that a plan?

Plan: a scheme or method of acting, doing, proceeding, making, etc., developed in advance. Example: *battle plans*.

I often feel like I am battling life without a plan—just taking it blow-by-blow, bracing myself for impact.

≥•

I didn't plan to throw away the box from my ex-husband, unopened. But then I chucked that plan as I chucked that box in the dumpster behind my apartment.

At first, when I received the seventeen-pound surprise from

the kind UPSer, I thought it was a box of yarn a friend had shipped to me. Then I saw the sender's name—Ex-Husband—and it took me a few moments to understand what was going on. Like a familiar face I couldn't quite place, there was a moment of failed brain recognition in which I didn't register the meaning of those eleven letters. His name. Having blocked all modes of communication with him a few months prior, it'd been a bit since I'd seen that specific combination of those eleven letters. They looked odd.

Ex-H and I divorced six months ago and after a few futile attempts at dating, we finally retreated to our own corners, planning never to hear from one another again. Now, a seventeen-pound surprise.

Plus an envelope with my name on it taped to the outside of the box.

The order of my thoughts as I held my Ex-H's box:

1. Did he ship me a dead animal?
2. Maybe his decapitated head is inside like in that movie *Se7en*.
3. The letter must be a suicide note.
4. Oh! It's probably just my books I let him borrow the last time we sex-rendezvoused. Sweeeeet!!!

Upon updating my sister and friend about the surprise present that I figured was meant to manipulate some feelings of guilt within of me, they both replied real quickly with similar responses.

Sister: "Don't open it. Did you hear about what happened in Austin yesterday?"

Friend: "Don't open it. Packages with bombs in them exploded in Austin yesterday. Two people died."

Looking at the packing label, I saw that the box was shipped from him—a resident of Austin—yesterday.

I considered things.

Like how Ex-H was totally capable of gifting me explosives.

Like how that thought didn't surprise me.

Like how his raging tendencies (mixed with my simmering and stubborn and suppressed anger) played a part in our marriage's blow-out. How it blew up.

Um.

Curiosity. Cat. That whole thing.

Thus: the unopened, unplanned *chuck*.

છ

Also,

Plan: a representation of a thing drawn on a pane, as a map or diagram.

One could say my suicide fantasies are a representation of a thing. The *thing* being how much I can't stand that I'm alive right now. That for sure is a *thing* that's been going on with me lately.

Perhaps, considering the current suicide considerations, it's a good *thing* I don't know how to draw, map out, or diagram plans of any kind. I don't know how to plan shit, including the structure of a day.

"I have a history of being scared to go to sleep," I inform my imaginary therapist.

She doesn't ask me why or when I've been scared to go to

sleep, because I already know the why and the when and if you're going to talk to yourself, you shouldn't have to have conversations about things you already know. Being border-line psychotic should at least consist of conversations that are interesting and about self-discovery or something. Or at least ones that lack redundancy.

"Maybe I'm just really depressed."

"Duh," imaginary therapist points out. "You're grieving."

Which is true. Because even though I'm glad the box and its contents are not weighing too heavily on me—no chuck regrets—there's still something I'm mourning. A shatteredness. Unfulfilled expectations. (Safety. Respect. Communication. Etc.) How we were supposed to love each other for forever, make a home together, make a duo life, protect it from the world's woes, and be a source of safety and companionship for each other. Marriage is a promise, a statement that *this is it.* That there isn't anyone else out there with whom I want to grow senile.

That didn't happen. I don't quite know how to quit things easily, though. Like life. I can't even come up with a plan for quitting life. I guess that's about indecision. I don't know. Either way, I'm usually a fucking trooper.

And so my weak heart beating with a grief I'd rather not know leaves me feeling a little lifeless.

"I just don't know how to live without him."

"But you also didn't know how to live with him." That's the imaginary inner voice of reason talking.

"Ergo, my not wanting to live?"

"If you slept more, I bet you'd have a more upbeat perspective on singledom."

Unlike the rest of the human species, when I get depressed, I sleep less. It's about that surprise moment when I wake up, eyes opening to the reality of another day I have to face. Dread keeps me from my bed, because if I don't go to sleep, then I won't have that moment.

"You know," imaginary therapist says with her *you're a dumbass for not thinking about this yourself* expression, "another option would be to figure out how to live differently."

"Like?"

"You need a plan for living."

Realization: if I had a suicide plan, I might not actually feel suicidal. Having a plan means having some sort of progressive logic. Means believing in a forward sequence of *things*. A movement of this and then that.

1. I will leave my house.
2. I will drive to a tall building.
3. I will park my car.
4. I will go to the roof.
5. I will jump.

Now that sounds like a plan.

All boxed up and ready to go.

৵

Though not a guarantee, here's what the box probably contained:

1. Aforementioned books

2. The coffee mug we stole from the bed and breakfast we stayed at on our wedding night
3. The framed pictures from our wedding
4. The framed picture of us looking all love-blissed and shit, standing under the huge tree he planted at the city hall in his hometown when he was ten.
5. Fucking raccoon and squirrel statues that were at one point cute and quirky but now seemed childish in the aftermath of a failed marriage
6. Stray clothes left behind when I moved out

What I *know* the box contained:

1. Nothing I needed
    a. I mean, I moved out a year ago and haven't been missing anything since. (I don't know if I'm talking about tangible objects or the dynamics of our marriage here. Probably both.)
2. Objects as fuel for an essay
    a. I was thinking I would write an essay about the box that would use whatever items were inside of it as an inventory of sorts, each item acting like a trailhead to relay an experience that would create an essay about marriage. Or rather, its failure. Unpack all of that. That essay was going to use the relics of my ruined marriage to say something larger about a shattered sense of independence, about the way you have to tear a relationship out at the seams to get back your own swatch of identity, re-possess some fabric

of sanity. Books, coffee mugs, knick-knacks, photos, and mementos from inside jokes. Those would be the objects my essay would use to begin its exploration.

In regard to that last item: I think we're doing just fine without them. I don't need anything from Ex-H to help me write an essay. He's already given me plenty of writing material, such as:

1. Lack of emotional well-being (and its domino effect)
2. The effects of an unattended-to schizoaffective disorder (his)
3. Financial instability (a problem of which we held joint custody)
4. You cannot force someone who is currently having a deep conversation with someone else in their head to talk to you (no matter how many tantrums I threw)
5. Paranoia (his, not mine. See #2.)
6. Impatience (mine, not his. See #4.)

All I need from him hasn't changed in the past six months since our official separation: space so we can keep aiming to go our separate, healthier ways.

The box, then, was surely full of clutter. Of what I left when I left. Of nicked-up knick-knacks. Of pictures no longer picture-perfect.

A seventeen-pound package of marital debris.

ॐ

My imaginary therapist has taken the lead in my support system. Phone tree for emergencies, she's at the top, the one I call the most when my brace-for-the-blows life approach is ineffective.

If I had a "real" therapist, I'd talk to her. But self-employed freelance editor + pre-existing condition = no affordable health care.

My imaginary therapist does sliding scale for me. We barter, actually. I'll talk to her and even though I don't listen to her advice, she has yet to give up on me because without me, she wouldn't exist.

Ex-H's solution for mental health issues was a phone app. A therapist app, actually. "Woebot," I shit you not. It texts you three times day, asking formulaic questions and offering you to check a pre-determined response box. That's your little bout of daily therapy.

Because of course the best way to work through the difficult, straining, super-complex human emotions that you're drowning in all over the place is via interactions with artificial intelligence. Swipe them woes away. Though I guess a touchscreen is involved so maybe it's the "touch" part that provides a type of physical, therapeutic contact with a tangible thing. It's practically a hug.

At least my imaginary therapist isn't separated from me by algorithms. She's in me.

If you listen, the gut speaks.

Which is where he kicked me.

Violence wasn't supposed to be a part of this—this marriage.

Though I guess that's obvious. Or should be. A given. Usually you don't go into marriage expecting to one day find yourself being abused. You don't plan on a physical assault. Don't foresee emotional manipulation.

What for sure for reals for sure was *not* in the box:

- A resolution
- Closure

Because even now, the day after I shoved the seventeen pounds into the green dumpster, I still cry. Sob. Wonder not what was in the box, but fissure over the fact of its existence. That marriage ended in shipped shrapnel.

What I mourn the most is the fact that the box could be filled. That is, memories were made, love was felt, and objects took on meanings of different memento-worthy moments. I miss the confidence that at least one part of my life was figured out—I had someone who would plan out a future with me. I lament the pledge of someone being there for me—that someone has my back. That I'm not facing this world alone. We could get each other out of our respective depressions and bring some encouragement and inspiration to get through the tough moments. But then we became each other's tough moments.

There were warning signs like how there are always warning signs you can't see until you've reached hindsight. Or you see them, but choose not to read them. Or can't quite comprehend them because surely the raging anger that fueled a kick was a fluke.

ew

"I don't know if I really want to kill myself," I tell imaginary therapist, "but everything that I love is gone and I'm just tired of hanging on."

"Your life has become a country song."

She smirks at her own wit and in my head we briefly bask in the comic relief.

Then she tells me what I don't want to hear.

"He kicked you, proving he was capable of hurting you in ways you never thought possible. You had to leave."

But he would never hurt me.

But then he did.

The relationship game rules were officially revised when foot struck stomach one night, twice.

"What would you tell your friend if she was considering dating her abusive ex?"

I don't answer. My reply is obvious.

And yet it took me six months to leave.

And yet it took a handful of re-dating attempts to know that I wanted to leave.

And how violence can't be a part of this—my self-care. Staying in the marriage, in a post-divorce relationship with him had become an act of self-harm.

Still, the grief. The missing him.

❧

I actually doubted there was a bomb inside, but I didn't doubt if Ex-H was capable—morally and logistically—of mailing out bombs. I know now that he's just that angry, just that smart, just that kind of crazy when he's not taking his psych meds. Last time I saw him, about two months prior to the box's arrival, he told me he stopped taking his anti-psychotics and that he had bought a shotgun.

We're all full of surprises.

Like when I shoved him once. Well, lunged at him. I think my bag was in my hands. We were sitting on a couch when he said something offensive about my mother. A statement full of disrespect. The bag was in my lap—I remember this now—and I just lunged. Blind rage. So angry. I needed to throw something. So I threw my body at him. Not passionately. Well, maybe passionately with a vengeance. And because I have terrible body–world coordination, I didn't even land on him. I tripped, my body tipped over and I spilled onto the couch cushion inches away from the intended target.

Later, he would claim this moment was an assault.

Later, he would say I was emotionally abusive and so when he kicked me because I was yelling at him and asking him why he hated my family, it was self-defense.

Four months later, I would finally get out of there.

Four months after that, finally the divorce would be finalized. That was the plan. Then post-divorce, things went awry and the unthinkable thunk itself into reality. Divorcees dating.

Life is full of surprises.

First, the surprise was that he kicked me.

Next, the surprise was that I didn't leave immediately. Or permanently. That I kept coming back.

Then, a good chunk of months later, the total surprise of eventually becoming thankful of the kick—though the reaction was more of a gradual transformation than instantaneous gratitude, it's the kick that kicked into gear my desire to kick him out of my life. The real kicker is that I went back, lesson not learned. Bad habits are hard to kick. It's challenging to quit something so intoxicating, regardless of how poisonous it is. How toxic he was. How we always forget the hurt first.

I wonder about what experiences my gut believes are worth remembering.

What artifacts are worth keeping.

৵

I know of that whole thing about insanity and its spawning from repetition. Doing the same thing over and over again, expecting different results. That's crazy.

"Why did you go back to him a few months ago?" That's imaginary therapist pushing me again with a valid question.

"Because he was doing well." That's my valid response if I only think about my decision in terms of "in that moment." Ex-H was one of those people who got in a really bad mental space—suicidal thoughts and whatnot, like my bad mental spaces—then he would get on meds when living felt too intolerable, then when he started to feel better again, he decided he was doing good and so who needs meds?

Obvious point he obviously never understood: IT'S THE MEDS THAT MAKE YOU FEEL BETTER.

Same thing. Over and over again. Emotions and mental states wildly oscillating. Unstable brain. Same actions. Same results.

Five years of this.

Yet he kept getting off his meds.

Yet I keep going back to him.

"Why?"

"He was doing well. Maybe it would stick that time."

But the only thing that sticks is my commitment to not accepting reality.

Like the reality that it wasn't too far-fetched of a suspicion that he gifted me seventeen pounds of explosives. Like the reality that I don't believe I'll ever really love life without him in it.

I'm just as stuck as he is. But I don't call my actions crazy. My term for them is love.

"That's crazy." Again with her valid points. "You need to start believing in what your *own* life, without him, can be like. Start desiring that shit for me, k?"

That's what's most surprising in all of this—the power of self-persuasion. Delusion. How I'm really good at lying to myself. Superb, actually. We're supposedly not able to tickle ourselves in the same way we aren't able to boo the hiccups out of us. But now, a year after my divorce, I surprise myself every day when I look back at how I told myself that "this is love." That, "sticking with it" was what marriage was all about. Scary how marriage is an excuse for learning to love what hurts you.

The sway of this delusion could have led me to open a box. And yes that could have led to my death, but living without him at times felt like a kind of death.

Either way, box unopened. Sometimes I grieve this, feeling like I threw everything away—him, our marriage, hope. Or I feel like if I wasn't grieving, wasn't feeling a bit suicidal-y, then I would have had the emotional strength to face whatever memories were in that box.

"Even if it was a bomb? Is he really worth dying over?" Imaginary therapist's eyebrows rise. "You say you don't know how to live without him, but if you really wanted to die or if you really wanted to be with him, which, let's face it, is its own kind of death, and if you truly thought you couldn't live without him then—"

"Oh fuck," I interrupt.

[Dramatic pause.]

Then I say it before she can:

"Then I would have opened the box."

ctrl + alt + delete

Consider yourself a task I have ended. Our relationship, a 404 not found. Our connection now disconnected. You, a broken link I wish I had been forbidden to visit, a threat I did not initially detect. You became a virus in my system, and I had to malware you out of it. I have now completed the uninstallation process, have reset my life's device back to its original settings from before five years ago when I mistakenly trusted your download of lies. So good luck spamming your way into someone else's unregistered trust—I have already reported your corrupted files.

Puppy Love

The Internet says that "puppy love," also known as a crush, is an informal term for feelings of romantic or platonic love, often felt during childhood and early adolescence. It is named for its resemblance to the adoring, worshipful affection that a puppy may feel.

I got a puppy because I was lonely. It's easier to purchase another species of animal than to make a human friend.

The puppy isn't a substitute for a child.

That's not true.

Long story short:

In a non-creepy way, I fell in love with my bff's four-year-old daughter when I helped to take care of her for a year. Then I cut out the bff from my life because this was right after my divorce when I was reading a book about how to heal from emotional abuse, and eventually I realized the book was describing my bff's treatment of me even more so than my ex's. After one too many silent treatments because I called out my bff on some major BS, I cut her off, unintentionally then slicing the four-year-old out of my life. I hadn't known how wonderful a child could be, the special kind of love you feel for a person whose life you're in charge of protecting.

Sans husband and four-year-old and bff, I got suicidal that year.

I felt lonely.

Thus, puppy.

Enter: Skylar (the Texas Cattle Dog)

৵

Skylar's restless. Her ten-week-old body paces the bed in circles, digs madly at the fitted sheet, then lies on me. Groans. Whines until I give her what she wants—my fingers to chew on. Every night, this struggle. Every night, I cede to her so that, pain be damned, she'll shut up already and fall asleep.

Fact: Human finger chewing is a violent form of toddler thumb sucking.

The puppy that was supposed to improve my life starts out by doing the opposite. She was supposed to calm me down, to be a pleasant distraction from my loneliness, and generally contribute to the quality of my life. But no: bursts of barking energy at 3:00 a.m., finding ways to jump up six feet up into the air to grab my flip flops from a shelf and chew them to slobbery bits, uses my apartment as her personal toilet, uses her leash as a tug-of-war toy, and how $500 worth of knitting needles are apparently the best chew toys, and even more so how the computer bag I got to replace the other computer bag she chewed up is apparently—for reals—the best chew toy *ever*. The puppy is failing me, adding to my sad existence.

ॐ

My bff's prema-silent treatment shouldn't come as a surprise. It's her go-to move whenever someone pisses her off, regardless of the offense. Still, a few days after I realized ditching the ex-bff meant ditching her daughter, I texted her, asking to see the girl. No reply. Waited a week. Sent another text. No reply. Six months of this weekly one-sided conversation. Loneliness amplified with each silent non-reply.

ॐ

Puppy love is for the juvenile. It's about being young and totally in love with a person who amazes you in every possible way and they can do no wrong and you worship them. That's how I felt about my ex-husband until a year after I became his wife. We were married for five years.

My ex-husband forbade me from calling him immature. Something about it being judgmental and a cut-down to his manhood, which—hi irony—is an immature way of navigating the world. That's not a judgment—that's a fact. A prime example of *immature*'s definition.

If only his immaturity was puppy-cute. Far from it. Though I would get those glimpses of the awesome husband I hoped he could be. They quickly retreated, though. Character flaws coming out again, head-first. Headstrong. Emotional abuse is not cute.

ॐ

I then began emailing the ex-bff, hoping the texts went un-replied because she had blocked my number. I made monthly requests. After a few days of each un-answer, I got depressed even more. Sobbed about the lost four-year-old.

Six more months of this. Silence.

That's when I got a puppy to fill the void.

My eye is twitching right now, which is Wikipedia-explained proof that I keep my life in a steady not-balance of chaos and stress and functioning and even breathing feels hard. Because after being a puppy mama for a few months now, Skylar has yet to be a good companion, has yet to help me de-stress.

But I don't have any other companions. The husband is gone, the bff is gone, the girl is out of my life, my family is either far away or nearby but doesn't really talk to me, I lack friends, I work from home and therefore lack work buddies, the Circle K clerk who knows my brand of cigarettes feels like the person in my life who knows me best—he's often the only human contact I have each day—and now I'm avoiding the puppy, who I got to make me feel not-lonely, as I go outside and hide from her on my balcony so I can knit alone because yarn doesn't yelp at you.

"This dog sounds like she's stressing you out," Circle-K clerk says. "Maybe it's just not a good fit. You could always get rid of her."

I hadn't thought about that because that's not an option. Yes, she has chewed up my books, knitting needles, windowsills, shoes, rocking chair, end table, face, etc. But a puppy is a com-mitment and I'm stubborn has hell—which is probably why

I was in a five-year marriage that pretty much sucked for the last four years of it. Plus, Skylar isn't a four-year-old girl whose mother bars me from seeing her and my therapist who I rarely see says it's good to be positive about things, so I guess that's a positive—she's still a cute puppy and not a source of grief. Just frustration. Like my ex-husband.

Text message to my mother the morning after a night full of barking and chewing that made the Circle-K clerk's suggestion start to feel like an option: "I think she is emotionally abusing me. Ruining the things that are important to me, demanding my attention, making me be responsible for all of her meals, I'm constantly having to placate her, and she controls how long I can be away from her and out in the world. Jesus Christ. That sounds like my ex-husband."

Ex-Husband	Skylar
Interfered with pursuing my writing passion	Destroys things important to me
Controlled how much time I spent with others	Controls my schedule
Did not play well with others	Enjoys barking at everyone near me
Kicked me	Bites me
Caused me to cry a lot	Licks my face when I'm crying about how shitty of a puppy she is
Didn't recognize and/or understand why I cried so much when he was off his psych meds and treating me like shit	Protest shits in the apartment when I'm not giving me enough attention

In the waiting room of her therapist's office, the four-year-old and her mother enter. I am there by surprise, the girl having no idea her mother and I were texting plans about rides and schedules and who would drive the girl back to kindergarten.

The four-year-old sees me, begins to squeal, "Miss Chelsey! Miss Chelsey! Miss Chelsey! Yayyyyyyyy!" She giggles and claps, her blonde little girl ponytail bouncing as she jumps.

I met the girl after my divorce. I hadn't seen her mother in years. My re-kindled friendship happened to happen during my marital split. Now that I had lost all of that love for my supposed "forever" person, I threw myself into helping with the girl, the object of my love shifting—though granted it was a different kind of love. A maternal love—a different kind of undying love. Taking care of a child is a wonderful distraction from grief. The girl, I guess, was my rebound.

Perhaps a type of transference.

And now I need a rebound from losing the girl.

The first night I had Skylar, I dreamt of the four-year-old. The puppy re-flipped the switch of my crushed maternal instincts.

❧

I hold her like a toddler—her freckled belly flat against mine, a big hug as she gets to work licking my nose and mouth until I almost suffocate. I keep my eyes open, though. Stare at the freckled snout that leads to her eyes, her ears pulled back, the paw that claws my face trying to bring my head closer to hers, which is when she rips a gash in the bridge of my nose. I take a picture of my puppy-mauled nose and send it to my only friend who says: "Ouch. Puppy autograph of puppy piranha?"

My reply: "Pawtograph."

Because why not portmanteau the way my puppy gnaws on and claws at me? It's funny. Something good must come out of this—positivity, Chelsey!—and funny is good.

§

Knock on my door. Puppy expectedly starts the barking thing. I open the door, non-violently (mostly) kicking puppy back.

"Hey, I'm with pest control."

"Okay."

"The landlord said you had a pest problem."

[Skylar tries running out of the front door. I grab her before she can.]

"Umm. Nope."

"Really?"

"Yeah."

[Puppy barks.]

"So you don't have any pest issues?"

[Skylar starts nipping at me.]

"Well I do have this puppy that chews on my face."

§

I went back and forth on whether I should get a dog.

When we were married, my husband and I were both not too enthralled with the idea of having kids. We considered ourselves selfish—we didn't want a tiny human to keep us from doing anything we wanted to do, whenever we wanted to do it. But then we would think about how a miniature combination of our genes might be kind of cute—though the kid would be brain-doomed because of a history of alcoholism and mental illness on both sides of the gnarly family tree.

Ultimately, though, what convinced us not to have kids was the indecisiveness itself. We didn't want to have a kid and then regret it. There's no (ethical) way of taking back that decision.

I went through the same thought process when considering getting a dog. I didn't want to get one then be like, "Yeah never mind. Return, please."

But then I had a moment of "whatever, let's just do this," and somehow thought that getting a puppy would be better than an adult dog because then I could train her.

But similar to children, puppies don't always do what you want them to do, nor do they become the perfect angel being that you hoped for.

ﻦ

Before the divorce, there was love—a lot of love. I adored the man I married and worshipped him and his affection for me. An unrelenting love, one that felt sturdy, deep. Not a trivial puppy love, but something lasting.

It lasted until I got to know him and his management of his mental illness (deny deny deny) and his narcissism and I saw how quickly love can un-flood me, retreat.

ﻦ

Though also how love quickly floods into me.

The girl held my hand while crossing every street.

Skylar hides under my legs when she's uncertain of the world.

The girl sat on my lap every chance she got.

After circling around and digging at the fitted sheet, Skylar curls her head into my neck to sleep.

Transference.

ॐ

Arriving home ritual:

I open the front door, step into my apartment and declare, "Where is my cute puppy?"

Skylar rushes to me from the bedroom, puppy ears flopping like mad. She lunges into my lap and whines as if telling me the story of her alone time. Whining in a good way. A squeal. The sound of excitement when there is a language barrier.

"And then what did you chew on?" I ask as she whinnies all cute puppy high-pitched.

"And then what did you do?" She whines away the stories of her day until all the excitement is squealed out of her, and she flops down on her back for her tummy to be rubbed, greeting then finished.

ॐ

It's hard to move on from the girl, but I'm starting too. I used to cry and cry because of grief and regret. Although now I have someone to console me—a pet. A Skylar. As she begins to inch away from puppyhood, I begin to inch away from my grief over the girl. The grief over the divorce ended months ago, so getting over how much I miss this girl has been a harder task than moving on from the five years of an emotionally abusive marriage. Skylar has finally started to help. She licks up my lingering tears, lies on me, paws at my lap now instead of my face. Making me feel less lonely, she is finally starting to fulfill her puppy duties.

Recently, I realized it had been a while since I contacted my ex-bff to see if I could see the four-year-old. Months, I believed. Curious as to just how long it had been since my last see-the-girl request, I search my email to see when that last communication attempt was sent.

March 18, 2019.

The day Skylar was born.

&

I'm curious if this is really a case of puppy love's reverse. How my insides squealed and giggled and clapped every time I saw the four-year-old. How I (the elder) got googly eyes when I saw the object of my affection (the youngster). How she could do no wrong.

How even though she can do a lot of wrong, I have started to squeal and giggle with Skylar as she starts to grow out of her chewing phase and is trotting into the land of good companion—a being I want to have around me.

One thing about puppy love is its trivial trait. Puppy love isn't supposed to be real love. But I do love my puppy (her cuteness keeps her alive), and I loved the four-year-old. No one else really understood the love I had for that girl. As if new-found maternal instincts—that love—is trivial.

None of this love is trivial.

I look at Skylar. She's sleeping at my feet, the tip of her nose resting on the tip of my toes. I don't have any reason to keep sitting here after this sentence.

I stay where I'm at. That's love.

Flash Flood

I put Courtney's shoes outside. Yesterday, the storm cleaned them. It was a nice gesture from whomever makes these things happen—the same whomever that made Courtney's shoes caked in her mother's blood. Her now-dead mother's blood. Still, the rain was an appreciated after-thought. Because whomever makes these things happen is trying to make up for making a daughter hold her mother in her arms as she bled to death. Blood coughed up, spewed out. A fatal flood of it.

I know these details and some others I wish didn't exist. I know that it took me ten paper towels to swipe away just the small splatters—dead mother reminders—from the dresser, which is to say nothing of what the rest of the bedroom looked like. I know that a few days after her mother's unexpected death, when Courtney held the shoes she was wearing that night of the sudden flood of too much blood, her body then thundered with unstoppable sobs.

Flashback.

I held her, then put her shoes outside.

I know that I'm angry at whomever decided to make these things happen. And I know that no storm can wash away the memories, even if the downpour cleansed the blood-caked shoes so Courtney didn't have to. So I didn't have to. Sure, a nice gesture, but really, you've done enough.

Paddling

Before Tulsa was put down around noon, she went down in the morning. A deaf, mostly blind, malnourished, twenty-four-year-old horse got on her knees at some point early in the a.m. and was lying on her side by the time the cops arrived. Neither of the two officers was the cop who showed up last week in response to an animal report. That cop will do a follow-up in a few weeks. These cops were responding to a new call. Apparently the neighbors have noticed some things.

Tulsa was being unintentionally starved. Accidental neglect. A lot has been going on 'round these parts—this six-acre property out in the middle of nowhere, Texas. Eleven deaths in eight months. Two cats, five chickens, two goats, a horse, and one mother all dead in the past 195 days. I did the math. That's an average of one death every 17.1 days.

After her mother died and one goat died and two cats died, Courtney, the official property owner of the now neglect-riddled ranch, found an oar in the chaotic clutter of her spider-webbed and dirt-coated barn. The oar was the perfect opportunity to paint and decorate a thing to express how she felt at that point. Art therapy of sorts. She glued some letters on it. "SHIT CREEK," it reads. The oar is hanging outside her bedroom door where Courtney's mom bled to death in her arms 195 days ago.

So with a mother dying and cats dying and goats dying and chickens dying and a dog dying during these past eight months, the horses fell to the wayside. They were put to pasture, left to fend for themselves, to graze on the brittle grass and drink from the muddy pond. Out there, they were forgotten about more often than not. It's the "not" that led to Tulsa turning skeletal. That led to the neighbors making calls. Too malnourished, too old, too many pre-existing health conditions, the horse is now a corpse.

A green tarp is draped over her body as we call an organization whose specialization is hauling off dead horses and is called—get this—Final Ride.

Earlier this afternoon, before I helped Courtney cut off the hair on Tulsa's lifeless tail—a common keepsake among country-living folk—I watched the vet stick so many drug-filled needles in Tulsa's neck that blood oozed out of the new wound. She took a long time to die. Courtney says that horse was always stubborn. Finally, there were a few final grunts. The heartbeat stopped, and her lungs and nerves twitched themselves until there wasn't enough life in Tulsa to keep twitching.

Her ribs were clearly visible. Hipbones jutting out just so, that they reminded me of supermodels because when it's not in reference to animals, malnourishment in our society is sexy. Approved of. Praised. This is more than appalling.

Though it is not as appalling as how the high, sharp peaks of Tulsa's hipbones arrived because of forgetfulness and distraction—a common thing 'round here now that Courtney's mom suddenly and unexpectedly left her daughter to fend for herself.

Grab your oar.

Tulsa's death was inevitable—all deaths are. But like Courtney's mother, Tulsa, too, died too soon. Even though a sixty-nine-year-old woman isn't the youngest thing, and neither is a twenty-four-year-old horse, they're still young enough to assume there are a good number of life years left. Their final ride doesn't seem so close. But life isn't a certainty.

The day my dog and I moved into Courtney's house to keep her company was the day Codi died in his doghouse. Heatstroke, I suspect. Another issue of neglect. And so on the day a puppy arrived on this property, the four-year-old dog who was living here left.

There was an equal amount of animal arrivals and departures that day.

There have almost been as many departures in these past 195 days as there have been survivors.

The survivors: ten cats, two horses, two chickens, one duck, two dogs, and one daughter. Eighteen life-sustainers. Though staying-aliveness is obviously not a given in this house.

Along with humorously decorating discarded oars, Courtney recently discovered a new crafting obsession—fake floral arrangements. There's something to say here about the certainty you feel when you know—without a doubt—that something won't die on you.

The fake flowers hanging around the house haven't died.

Yet.

ॐ

Final Ride finally arrived. It's been two days. Two days of the tarp draped over the dead horse. Two days of sun crashing down on the covered corpse. Two days of decomposition, and so when we pull the tarp off Tulsa, I'm surprised by how much better she looks. Her gut is bloated, and aside from the sack of whatever that is hanging outside her ass and is filled with liquid and please God don't let that thing pop, she looks good. Not a rib in sight.

Never did I ever think I'd watch a woman wrap a cable around a dead horse's neck and pull the horse—its eyes still open, dead blue orbs piercing my vision—up onto a flatbed trailer, like it's a car being towed. Within minutes, Tulsa is whisked away for her final ride to the horse cemetery and Courtney and I go back into the cluttered house to pretend we didn't just see that.

And now it's a few hours later, and Courtney and I are in the dining room talking about whatever when Skylar, my dog, starts barking ferociously at the closed blinds that cover the sliding glass door that leads out to the backyard.

"What the hell are you barking at, dog?"

Probably Casey, the half-German shepherd and half-great Pyrenees who lives in that back section of the yard. I peek my head through the slats to assess what Skylar is barking at. I don't see her at first but then, oh look. There's Casey. The top of her big white head poking up from the other side of the deck, and there are her big black eyes, staring right into mine.

Unblinking.

She's still staring.

And there's the chain she's tied to, wrapped around the post of the railing. A sliver of her pink collar seen.

She's still staring.

Unblinking.

Chain. Collar. Post. Four-feet-tall deck. Just the top of her head poking out.

And those eyes still staring at me.

Unblinking.

Click.

"Casey's not okay!" I scream.

The horror doesn't end there. It doesn't end when Courtney rushes through the door. It doesn't end when she screams, "Casey!" Or when I ask, "Is she okay?" even though I know the answer. Or when Courtney says, "She's dead," and I put my dog in her kennel and go back out to Courtney who is sitting on the deck steps, sobbing.

The horror doesn't end when I see Casey's stiff body on the ground after Courtney unclasped her collar and she thunked down—it only gets stronger when I notice the bloody chew marks in the side of the deck, right next to where her head was.

There is no end to this horror because I will never be able to un-see those desperate, bloody bit gouges in the wood, the blood on dead Casey's teeth. And I can never un-see those eyes, unblinking. Her final look as she gasped out her final breath—pleading.

Courtney and I consider the timeline. Neither of us heard her struggling, so she must have died before we came back into the house. Which is to say that as we were watching a dead horse get winched up onto a flatbed trailer, a dog was getting hanged to death on the other side of the house.

Math update: twelve deaths in eight months.

That's one death every 16.1 days.

Skylar barks from her kennel—it's music to me. It means she's alive—which is apparently is an extraordinary feat to achieve in this house. Her barking breath is a reassurance. Never have I ever loved her barking as much as I do now.

ॐ

Courtney's mom died and now Courtney's animals are dying because she doesn't know how to live. I look at the squalor all around me. The way I must brace myself for another death. Or steady myself so I don't trip over the messes that list to the left. Piles of junk swaying to the right. Everything is everywhere and so Courtney's days are spent in a continuous cycle of questioning, "Have you seen _____?"

Her items are as lost as she is.

The main thing dying here is Courtney's spirit. And the effects of it are rippling out, literally killing everything around her. I think of the concept of a catalyst. Regina's death. Courtney's trauma. A short matrilineage of death. Courtney has no children, so next in line are the animals. They're dropping faster than the flies around here that circle the broken sink, the piled results of a hoarder, the fermented bag of grapes that was sitting on the counter for weeks. "I'm gonna clean it," Courtney declared. After another couple of weeks, I gave up on seeing her intentions come to fruition and I threw the mush and ooze of green grapes out, hundreds of gnats and dead fruit flies included.

There is so much that's going wrong here. These things shouldn't be happening. But they are. They keep happening. All I can wonder is when God will stop beating a dead horse.

The sunset is gorgeous tonight, by the way.

Beauty found in a diminishing thing.

A Slim Sexuality

After I was sexually assaulted, I lost twenty-two pounds and finally felt skinny enough to fuck a man. The almost-eating disorder that had been stewing inside me for more than a decade was exacerbated when a stranger grabbed me on the street, grabbed my pussy, grabbed whatever slim sense of security I had in this body that I've actually never liked. I had been a 137-pound lesbian since I came out at the age of sixteen and although not a single one of the gagilion body measurement scales, charts, tables, gauges, devices, calipers, apps, trackers, tapes, calculators, gurus or bod pods[8] would consider my weight "fat" for my height, pre-pussy-grabber, I had felt fat and decided to be all butch about it to survive the awkwardness that is a body. This isn't to say my normal-BMI-ranged physique made me a dyke, but that dressing butch and wearing baggier clothes a) hid my body, and b) helped me to feel masculine-sexy in the world of lesbos. See? Someone's gotta wear the cargo pants. I never considered my too-big-by-my-standards body could qualify to wear anything else.

---

[8] It's a thing. Google it.

In my head, dating women was a body competition. In size, that is. It wasn't something stated or discussed, but each night as my girlfriend slept next to me, I'd do my own assessment, cupping her stomach in my hand and wondering if the little lump of her lower belly was larger than mine. Or with my elbow on my hip, arm extended out, hand resting on the ridge of her hips, measuring their steeper rise compared to mine as I spooned her, feeling comfort in my hips being lower, supposedly smaller, though worrying that her peak was at a higher altitude not because she was bigger, but because I was heavier and dipping down into the mattress more than her slim bones, that the rise of my body was starting from below sea level.

Each night, a measurement as she slept. Each night, a failed attempt at reassurance because she always scored higher on the body assessment. Of course she did. I'm always the one who judges me most.

の

The assessment of scales. On a scale of 1–10 (1 being not at all, 10 being all the fucking time) how often do I think about my body, its form, its failure?[9] On a scale of 1–10, how often do I weigh my two options when it comes to what will make me feel more okay with my body in that moment—food or a cigarette?[10] On a scale of 1–10, how often do I actively attempt to scale the mountain of body hatred to reach the peak where perhaps I'll get a peek of what body acceptance could feel like?[11]

---

[9] 10—all the fucking time.

[10] 12—more than all the fucking time.

[11] 0—never ever will I attempt to love this mass. This mess. I'm lazy. And stub-

176 | Chelsey Clammer

I'm not strong enough for that accession to full-bodied acceptance.

This has to do with believing in myself.

Like how I never believe I'm skinny enough.[12]

❧

Panic attacks dispelled my pounds.

During the time when the twenty-two pounds were getting themselves gone post-assault, I initially got offended when people admired my body and said, "You're so skinny." I wanted to scream that they shouldn't praise the side effects of trauma. I wanted to be forthright and tell them that it's easy to be skinny: "Just have an eating disorder and get yourself sexually assaulted and you'll be set." I never said that because social etiquette.

People didn't expect me to say that like how now people don't expect me to say that trauma made me skinny and I don't necessarily mind it. Not that sexual assault is a healthy diet plan, but I stopped eating after a stranger grabbed me on the street, grabbed my pussy and said, "Hey baby what's your name?" I stopped eating after that because I figured the smaller my body, the less *me* there would be for the next *him* to grab.

Plus, dizzy with hypervigilance and anxiety, I didn't want to ground myself with sustenance. Dissociation is way easier

---

born. And that's my size—0—which confirms I'm skinny regardless if I believe it, which, in a weird way, is a type of body acceptance. I accept I am actually a size 0. I don't accept—and cannot see—that my body is small enough to fit into it. This is the insanity of having body dysmorphia.

[12] Odd how I approve of my clothing size, though not the size of my body. Welcome to my brain.

to achieve if you're already about to pass out from malnourishment.

So I moved on in life post-assault by leaving my body behind. I marched ahead with less of me and that's when I started to feel skinny enough to wear tight jeans. Skinny enough to be kinda femme. Shed enough skin to shed the baggy clothes and be body-confident enough to meet social standards of femininity to fuck a man.

Four years later, I would.

But first, nine years before I date him, we were roommates in college and he fucked one of our other roommates one night and I yelled at him the next morning, spewed feminist rhetoric fueled by a hangover because I was jealous and was secretly super-attracted to him and wished I was the one he had fucked. Later, when we're married, he'd tell me that he didn't try to fuck me that night because he knew I was a lesbian. How I interpreted that: I was too fat to fuck.[13] Really, though, he was just that respectful of a guy which means that maybe it's not that I wasn't skinny enough to fuck, but not bisexual enough. But in my head, I was too fat and butch to be straight-girl skinny.

---

[13] Before you hate me, let me make this clear: It's not that overweight people aren't desirable. All body types gorgeous and amazing and sexy. But my head doesn't feel that way about my own body. You see, I truly believe that bodies are beautiful and I know size doesn't define anyone's worth, but my eating disorder insists that's not true for me. My feminism knows that bodies are to be celebrated—my body dysmorphia forbids me from attending the party.

I heard more whistles after I was assaulted. Wearing tight jeans and halter tops, I got more comments. My body, un-hidden in tight clothes, started to feel like it was on display for praise.

Although I wasn't fishing for comments, their attention was flattering as fuck. If I was attractive enough to harass, then my body confidence went up, and my caloric intake kept going down. Even though I wasn't feeling anxious anymore because of the assault, I then had a body size I needed to maintain. But my desire didn't change with my wardrobe. Women were still my preference, though then I felt like I could be with someone more butch. For once, I could be the small one of the pair. Feeling oddly empowered by tight jeans, I didn't want to go back to being the baggy butch. And not once in all of my thinking did I realize that I didn't have to be skinny to be femme, even though I saw plenty of voluptuous femmes out there who were gorgeous. Never did I realize that could be me.

The male college crush and I hooked up nine years later when, at twenty-eight years old, I admitted my long-standing desire for him, regardless of my previous staunch belief that I was the gayest gay who ever gayed. I let go of my gold star lesbian status and allowed myself to finally give in to my desire for this man.

He was a small man with slim hips. 30 × 32 pants measurements. And yet even with *him*, even with his male physique that my femaleness could never match, as we started dating, my secretive nightly assessment of our hips' horizons began.

I didn't think I would do that with a dude. Apples to oranges, after all—women and their hips and men and their not-a-lot-there hips. But still, I measured our ridges and we had equal altitude. Prior to the assault, I had bought men's jeans for years. Then as I lost weight, my butch attire expired. But I remembered my size: 30 × 30. Looking at the tags on my boyfriend's pants, I was horrified. Retroactive shame. I cursed my past self for being so fat—as large as a man! I know this thought is absurd. With my MA in Women's Studies, I know there are many people of many sizes and of all genders and they are all beautifully majestic. I intellectually knew this, but I emotionally knew I was scared to gain weight and become larger than my soon-to-be husband. Were that to happen, were I to un-become straight-girl skinny, I wouldn't be able to hide behind a butch identity because now I had already deemed myself the femme. He wore the cargo pants, not me. If I gained weight, I was fucked.

ॐ

We got married after six months of dating. It felt right, secure, stable. My love for the man even helped to ground me some and lifted the final bits of anxious residue from the emotional mess of being assaulted. I started to be good to my body, even gained ten pounds. It felt okay because he felt okay to me—that he loved me and praised me and damn my neurosis, I didn't have to be a size 0 to be attractive to him.

And then things changed.

He started to get controlling, started to have unpredictable bursts of rage. Throwing objects, pounding on the dashboard of his car, screaming at me when he felt like someone else had done him wrong. A year into the marriage, my role of wife changed from being an equal and respected companion to having to pad the world for my husband for my own emotional safety.

As I lost my grasp of the empowered woman I considered myself to be, I started to do the thing I knew had worked for me in the past both to abate anxiety and to increase the survival skill of dissociation—I stopped eating.

Back to the anxiety diet plan.

At the four-hour mark, my body senses the countdown and my brain is consumed with anxious uncertainties. What mood will he be in when he gets home? Will he recognize I'm still working? Will he care? What office politics will he be pissed about today? How will he treat me tonight because of how he perceived others have treated him that day?

This is my marriage.

In four hours, he'll be home from work.

The countdown.

I can't concentrate with the anticipation of another dose of emotional abuse I know is soon to be served to me. It is always there, waiting.

Always. There.

Always there with the:

- Screaming
- Mocking
- Shaming
- Gaslighting

• And, once, kicking

As his abuse strengthens, I continue to lose what little appetite I had. I stuff my fear of him deep inside my body, letting it fill me up instead of food. Anxiety hidden within a size 0. Again.

Three hours, now.

Dissociation further settles in with my empty stomach. It's year three of our marriage and I've lost eighteen pounds.

Countdown to the putdowns. What did I do wrong this time?

I gave this man my love and he took away eighteen pounds of my body, squeezed them out of me with his skillful and expert role of anxiety-inducing enthusiast. The daily diet of emotional abuse.

At year five of our marriage, I'll be thirty-three years old and finally feel free.

৵

Text I sent to my friend when I received the email that contained a picture of the finalized divorce papers: "This might be TMI, but when I saw my divorce was finalized, I got really horny."

In fact, within four months after my divorce, I broke two vibrators. Freedom from emotional abuse felt gratifying. I could be me again and not worry about how I would be treated at the end of each day.

Free from the abuse, I could date whoever—the cute butch 7-11 clerk or the tall strong Shell Station dude clerk.[14] But

---

[14] All smokers know their gas station clerks pretty well because we interact with

again free from anxiety, I worried about gaining weight, fearful that I'd have to re-buy baggy clothes. Worried that without trauma helping to keep me skinny, I'd return to having to hide my 137 pounds of body.

৶

I give numbers a lot of weight. Lucky numbers that are more random than reasonable. Objective numbers outside the context of my eating disorder. We measure up the world numerically.

Then I measure myself up. The scales. Numbers have value, of course. Though now it is two years after my divorce and there is one number that doesn't mean anything to me: sixty-five.

That's my boyfriend's age.

You might be thinking that doesn't add up. I mean, really. It's a thirty-year age difference.

Even though I usually give hefty significance to digits, the fact of his six and five that tell me he's been breathing for three decades longer than me doesn't hold much weight.

Sixty-five is just a number.

Like how 137 is, in reality, just a number.

Unlike my ex-husband, my current boyfriend is enjoyable to be around. I feel seen by him, not seen as a thing he can let his frustrations out on. What a difference it is to want to stay present in every moment when the person you're around is making you feel like an actual person. One who's worthy of respect, of joy, of experiencing the poetry of skin when it's touched by hands that are in awe of it, not taking advantage of it.

---

them on a daily basis as we support our pack-a-day habit.

In his presence, the weight is lifted. Numbers become numbers again, un-signifying themselves and shedding the judgements and I am no longer a woman with a never-light-enough body, no longer letting physique steer my sexuality and self-acceptance. I am simply a woman with a body that she uses to tell his body that this here is love.

He tells me I'm beautiful and at first I tell him he needs to stop objectifying me. I consider the fact of my body, its slim size. He clarifies. It's not about that. Shows me the definition of beautiful.

It's about excellence.

Like what it is to be present in my body, to not have to hide anxiety or flesh, but to arrive in each moment with a *yes*. Yes—I want to be here with him, but more important, I want to be here with me.

This is beautiful.

છે♥

Fucking my three-decades-older-than-me boyfriend makes me feel good about my body. I worry this thought will make my boyfriend feel bad about his body. But I love his form. Every bit of it. Every way that every pore, mole, wrinkle, white hair, line and curve and angle and all of him is something I can smash myself against.

With him, my body shifts from shame factory and becomes its own language for us to connect with. Body comparisons are impossible.

I know it seems like this shift in me happened quickly. Like, bye abusive husband, hello new awesome boyfriend and BAM!

Eating disorder cured. But disorders aren't something to be cured. They're to be navigated. And with a respectful and Chelsey-positive boyfriend at the helm of this current sexuality journey, the insanities of my own mind/body split have calmed down a bit. This man isn't some solution, but the love he has for me and the care with which he treats me has helped me to see that my body isn't a problem. Not that I totally believe that, but his belief in it lessens some anxiety, helps me to feel safe in my skin again—to see my body as a thing that can be shared and explored, not a tool of emotional protection. All of this means my body's mass is no longer a strong obsession. Rather, it's just a part of me. Like those lingering insanities.

And so I feel safe. Even after surviving a sexual assault and an abusive marriage, I have finally found safety. And in this security, a sense of a strong body grows, regardless of a number.

ॐ

First, I came out as a lesbian at sixteen. (137 pounds)

Then I came out as a trauma survivor at twenty-five. (115 pounds)

Then I came out as a lesbian who married a man at twenty-nine. (125 pounds)

Then I came out as a divorced woman at thirty-three. (107 pounds)

Now, at thirty-five, I don't know how much I weigh but I do know that I come a lot because my sixty-five-year-old boyfriend is a champ in the sack and part of that is because our relationship is excellent—like me, apparently—and this isn't to say that I'm "cured" or that I'm telling the truth when I say I don't know how much I weigh,[15] but just that I'm now starting to see that my body isn't a thing I have to measure, isn't something I have to survive. It's a guide. So now instead of ditching my body and letting it declare my desirability, I'm inhabiting it, letting my body show me the way to where respect and pleasure—regardless of gender, regardless of numbers—get me to un-measure.

---

[15] 122 pounds—of course I own a scale. I have an eating disorder.

Acknowledgments

First and always, thank you to Kate Gale, Tobi Harper, and all of the Red Hen Press crew for supporting this book and being so dedicated to your authors. I love you people.

My friends and family sustain me, keep me going, and the writing wouldn't happen without them because 1) I wouldn't have a cheering squad telling me that I can do this writing thing, b) I wouldn't be alive and relatively sane without their support, and iii) being a nonfiction-er, I wouldn't have anything to write about it. My specific undying love and gratitude go out to Mindy Clammer, Marya Hornbacher, Angela Mackintosh, Melissa Grunow, Kate Buley, Sabrina Long, and Clayton Davis.

And then there are my editing clients and students. Y'all inspire me so damn much with your words and your passion. Laraine Herring, Lori White, Jackie Carter, and Linda Petrucelli—thank you for trusting me with your words and for reading mine. I also wouldn't feel as supported in this writing life if it weren't for being a part of the *WOW! Women on Writing* community. So thank you for existing.

Also, thank you to Naomi Kimbell and Dana Clark for providing excellent feedback on some of these essays and to all of the wonderful editors I worked with when preparing these essays for publication in their journals.

Patrick, thank you for helping me to detect my heartbeat again when I didn't know if that was possible.

And Tyler, thank you for keeping it going.

About the Author

Chelsey Clammer is the author of the award-winning essay collection, *Circadian* (Red Hen Press 2017), and *BodyHome* (Hopewell Publications 2015). Her work has appeared in *Salon*, *The Rumpus*, *Hobart*, *Brevity*, *McSweeney's Internet Tendency*, *The Normal School*, and *Black Warrior Review*. She teaches online writing classes with *WOW! Women On Writing* and is a freelance editor. Chelsey received an MFA in Creative Writing from Rainier Writing Workshop, and an MA in Women's Studies from Loyola University Chicago. She currently resides in Austin. You can read more of her writing at *www.chelseyclammer.com*.

CPSIA information can be obtained
at www.ICGtesting.com
Printed in the USA
JSHW052005240722
28459JS00005B/15